DIAMOND

DIAMOND

Al Kirkland

Copyright © 2013 by Al Kirkland.

Library of Congress Control Number:		2012924229
ISBN:	Hardcover	978-1-4797-7201-8
	Softcover	978-1-4797-7200-1
	Ebook	978-1-4797-7202-5

This book was printed in the United States of America.

To order additional copies of this book, contact:
Xlibris Corporation
1-888-795-4274
www.Xlibris.com
Orders@Xlibris.com
124031

CONTENTS

CHAPTER 1

Tony, a nine-year-old introverted boy, is awakened each morning with wet licks on his face from his dog, Magnum. After the wake-up licks, Magnum sits at the bedroom door and stares at Tony. This is his dog's wake-up call to let Tony know that he needs to go outside. Prior to letting him out, Tony sits on the side of his bed, picks up his family's picture, and reminisces about how two of his brothers died. Tony reflects on that afternoon.

He was coming home from school when two of his brothers approached him in a stolen sports car and told him to get in. He entered the backseat assuming that it was stolen, so he glanced out in all directions, looking for the police. As a police car passed them on the opposite side and made a sudden U-turn, he informed his brothers that they were being followed. *I should've kept walking*, was Tony's thought, knowing now that this quicker way home could lead to a quicker way to jail. When the flashing red lights came to life on the police car, the speed chase began. Tony put on his seat belt, not knowing the outcome of the ride until the car crashed into a truck. His two brothers were thrown from the car by the impact and died.

The dog becomes impatient and begins to bark. Tony reluctantly walks out the bedroom door and lets him out as his mother walks by, who tells him not to be late for school. She stresses again how important it is for him to stay in school since he is the younger of the two surviving children. His mother explains to him that his brother Ace will be home that same day from prison and that he should prepare himself for the celebration. The endless years, so it seems, have passed, and it is finally time for Tony's older brother Ace to leave the correctional institution where he has been incarcerated as a juvenile offender at the age of twelve.

Eighteen-year-old Ace has been incarcerated for attempted murder. He is sitting on the bench inside the juvenile facility, eagerly awaiting to be counseled by the parole board, which includes the assistant commissioner of corrections and three other members. While waiting, he's preparing mentally to acclimate himself back into civilian life in his neighborhood. Ace lies down on the bench, reflecting on how he got arrested and how his brother Antwon, who was with him at the time of the arrest, was shot by the police.

Antwon and Ace walked through an alley in Trenton, New Jersey, between East State Street and Walnut Avenue in the Wilbur Section in Trenton, New Jersey. Antwon saw a house where they knew the owners weren't home. Surprisingly, the back window was left slightly open. Antwon stopped and pointed toward the house, telling Ace that no one was home and that there was a fish tank with exotic tropical fish in it. They walked over to get a closer look through the window. After turning over a trash can, they took turns standing on top of it to look at the beautiful exotic fish swimming in a huge tank located in the dining room of the house. Ace was twelve years old at that time and was fascinated by the fish. Antwon tapped Ace's leg and told him, "I'm going inside," so Ace allowed him to get onto the can to gain access through the window. Antwon entered the house with Ace right behind him. Once inside, Antwon looked around while Ace stared at the fish. Antwon went upstairs, leaving Ace by the fish tank. Ace entered the kitchen and found a small can of fish food nearby to feed the fish. He was excited by the way they reacted to the unexpected treat, so he continued to feed them.

Antwon came back down the stairs with a clock radio in his arms. Ace looked surprised to see him with it and asked, "What else is up there?"

Antwon told him that he didn't know and put the radio down by the front door. Curiosity influenced them to go upstairs. Antwon, as always, took the lead. While upstairs, Ace went into the bedroom and looked under the bed, then under the pillow, where he found a handgun. He grabbed the gun, turned it over, and stared at it. Antwon, carrying a small television set, called to him, "Let's go!" Ace tucked the gun into the waistband of his trousers as he followed down the steps. As Ace walked back to the dining room, Antwon was by the front door retrieving the clock radio and putting it under his free arm. Ace was already at the back door, looking back to see what Antwon was doing. Seeing that Antwon was walking toward him at the back door, Ace pulled the gun out from his waist to stop it from falling down his pants. He held the gun at his side and opened the back door. As he opened the screen door and stepped outside, a plainclothes cop was kneeling by that same trash can the two brothers used to climb into the window. The cop hollered, "Freeze!"

Ace panicked, not knowing who the man was, and shot him in the chest, hitting the bulletproof vest before the officer could pull out his gun. Another cop shot at Ace and called on his radio, "Shots fired. Officer down."

Despite the distance, he barely missed hitting Ace. Ace ducked and ran back inside the house. Antwon was shocked and surprised from the gun battle as he dropped what he was carrying and ran to the front door. There, he was met by a hail of bullets from the waiting police officers as he ran out from the house. Ace panicked and ran back upstairs. The police surrounded the house and told Ace to surrender. Ace ran into the bedroom where he found the gun and locked the door behind him, thinking how his brother was shot. He grabbed the house phone and called his mother. Ace told her the vicinity where he was, not being sure of the exact address. She cried profusely as he illustrated to her how they shot Antwon and how the police shot at him too. Not knowing exactly where he was or what to do, a mother's instincts took over. She dropped the phone and ran out of her home in the general direction of where she thought her sons to be. As the police tried to decide whether or not to send the dogs in to locate Ace, his mother broke through the police line before the cops grabbed her. The captain told them to let her go. He then ordered her to bring Ace out with the gun in her hand, pointing it toward the ground. She ran inside the house and called her son. Ace heard her and ran back downstairs. After hugging him, she took the gun and convinced him to surrender into police custody. Holding Ace's gun as she was told, she led him outside. The police immediately took the gun, cuffed Ace, and placed him in the backseat of a squad car. His mother was allowed to ride in another patrol car to the police station.

After reflecting on his brother Antwon, Ace goes to sleep as he lies on the bench. Five minutes later, Ace is awakened by two corrections officers who aren't pleased to find him lying on the bench asleep in the holding area while he awaits his audience with the parole officers. One officer poked Ace on his right shoulder as he told him, "Hey, you ain't home yet. The board is ready to see you. Wait until you get home to get comfortable. Don't do it in my area."

Ace has always disliked cops or anyone in a police uniform because of his brother Antwon's death. So he stands up with his fist balled up and tells the officer, "Don't touch me and don't talk to me like that. Just because I'm leaving this place doesn't mean I won't see you on the streets. That way, we can touch each other without your boys around to protect you. I ain't touching you, so don't touch me. You ain't my father."

The officer's partner stands behind Ace, knowing that this situation could become violent. The officer who touched Ace is about twice his age. He looks him in his eyes and tells Ace in a sorrowful way, "Son, if I were your father, you wouldn't even be here."

Ace looks at him with an understanding of what has just been said and then holds his head down and walks into the boardroom with nothing else to say. While inside the boardroom, the board members introduce themselves to Ace. The board consists of four members: the assistant commissioner of corrections and three other men. The assistant commissioner starts asking him questions and tells him that his release is determined by the board because he shows that he matured a lot while incarcerated. He also tells Ace that his record indicates that he is on his way to rehabilitating himself. Also Ace is now eighteen years old, and this is the last year for him to legitimately enroll in high school. The assistant commissioner tells Ace, "Rehabilitation starts in here. Leaving prison doesn't mean that you're rehabilitated.

But if you can deal with the streets the way you handle yourself in here, by using your head, you could make it out there, young man. But the choice is yours. Whatever you do, just remember, prisons will always welcome you when you fail and resort to crime."

Ace nods his head to acknowledge what the commissioner has said, signs some documents, shakes their hands, and egresses from the room. Hours after his release, Ace's mother registers him for school at Central High.

The "no child left behind" mandate is in full effect at Central High. The Board of Education mandates that Central High transfer a maximum of twenty of their mentally challenged students to West Winsor High Charter School. It allows this school to transfer by bus special-needs students, incorrigible students, and ex-convicts. These students are what the principal considers rejects. But in order to make the "no child left behind" policy work, Central High is giving this privilege to educate them at West Winsor High Charter School. The school officials at Central High are discussing the mandatory busing policy to determine who will be bused. The principal and basketball coach are discussing about how they want the school to repeat the state's basketball championship. The basketball coach tells the principal in a diplomatic way that he doesn't want any of his ballplayers to be bused to another school. The principal tells the coach that he has no love for two of his ballplayers and that they must go. Those players are Bayshawn and Isaiah. These players are two of the most outstanding ballplayers on Central High's ball team. The coach reluctantly concurred and informed him about another player named Ace, who was coming from jail.

He didn't want him on his team either. He said that Ace would be a bad influence on the other teammates. The principal agreed and ended their conversation.

Ace and his mother enter the principal's office that afternoon. Ace is eager to resume his life in public school to help rehabilitate himself. After everyone is introduced, Ace talks to the principal about how Central High could benefit from his presence because of his athletic ability and his grade point average. The principal tells Ace that the decision has been made to transfer him to a charter school and that it was recommended by the basketball coach.

Central High won last year's state basketball championship, and it gave the school statewide recognition; so the coach's word is final. Ace puts his head down in disbelief. While incarcerated, he wanted to prove to himself that he could make a difference by doing something positive at Central. The principal explains to him that this is just one of many disappointments that he'll face. His mother cuts into the conversation to say that the positive difference will be made by her son regardless of which school he goes to because Ace is determined to succeed.

West Winsor High School is approximately fifteen miles from where Ace's family lives. It is a predominantly Caucasian township that has a court order mandate to integrate their high school for state funding. This diversified school system would generate more federal grants for the school board and enhance the mayor's image.

The principal at West Winsor High School, Mrs. Esteves, is determined to change the male-dominated coaching staff and put her female friends into all the coaching positions at her school. She has a meeting with her basketball coach and his assistant coach to inform them that she is replacing the coach with a woman since the team didn't win any games last season. When she asked the assistant coach to remain in his position as the assistant coach, they both giggle at the thought that a woman has better coaching skills than they have. The coach and the assistant coach begin to laugh out loud, ridiculing her decision and choice for a woman coach for the boys' basketball team.

After school, the newly hired basketball coach, Mrs. Wynn, discusses with her husband the job of coaching a boy's ball team and the aggravations that come with it.

Mrs. Wynn transferred from Shabazz High School in Newark, New Jersey, after buying a house in West Winsor, New Jersey. Her husband decided to leave the inner-city life in Newark, New Jersey, to settle in the suburbs of central New Jersey as he continues to teach in Newark by way of commute.

She states that the new job would display her talent in leading a team to a championship, against all odds. Her husband is the coach of Shabazz High School girls' basketball team, which is the number-one-rated girls' basketball team in the state of New Jersey, having won the state championship last season. The husband and wife joked about their coaching jobs and made a bet on who would win if their respective teams ever played against each other. After the joke, Mrs. Wynn thought seriously about scheduling a game with her husband's girls' team.

The next day, Ace learns that some of his boys will be transferred with him to West Winsor High, so he feels a little at ease. While walking around the neighborhood with his brother Tony, they reminisce on how things used to be in the Wilbur section of Trenton, New Jersey. Ace's friends see him on the street and congratulate him for being home. One asks him how long he is planning to remain out of prison. Ace's reply is that he is in a psychological prison and is trying to find his way out of his negative feelings toward life itself. "I'm a changed man, dude."

His friend then states, "Don't tell me you done found Jesus in prison too. I heard that he died and went to heaven. Are you saying that you've found Jesus in prison and you changed your ways? I guess that really makes you rehabilitated. So is you is, or is you ain't rehabilitated?"

Ace reflects on the books he read on rehabilitation and begins to talk like a man with a lot of wisdom.

"When I was locked up, it didn't give me a clearer understanding because my mind wasn't open. All I thought about was being out here on the blocks. And what I'll be getting into. Being out here in the open air around nature allows me to think more clearly about my opportunities. Like for instance an unborn baby or anything else that's unborn. It can't think clearly because it's confined. Even though it's alive, it's confined. But after it comes out of confinement, it begins to think a little more clearly. What little thought that's inside of that being, whether it's human or animal, it begins to think, or it uses instinct. And once it's around nature and people, it begins to think more clearly on how to express itself to achieve its goals in life. But feel me on this, if we don't spend time around nature, enjoying it while we're alive, we'll only be with nature when we die. Either six feet under or cremated and thrown in the ocean. Death is an eventuality. That's what King Solomon said, you feel me?"

Ace's friend looks at him, wondering who King Solomon is, but realizes that Ace just came out of prison, so it must be prison talk.

"Yeah, I know, that's right. Hey, I gotta bounce."

He gave Ace a half hug and walked away. Ace and Tony continue to walk before seeing his friends teasing a young lady named Fran'Sheila. She is introverted and the only child in her family. Ace and his brother walk by her and say hello. She looks at Ace, surprised that she has been spoken to in a polite way.

Fran'Sheila is the finest girl in the neighborhood and is very shy with much class. She is often hated on and taunted by most boys around the way. Ace wonders why she doesn't speak back. His brother later explains why she looked that way and tells him about her. They enter the neighborhood basketball court, where all the ballplayers welcome him back.

Life in the communities in the township of West Winsor is much slower than living in the hood. But criminal elements do exist. Joey, who is the neighborhood numbers taker and a senior student at West Winsor High, walks past the corner deli when the owner comes out to complain. "Joey, how come my number always comes out when I don't play it? Who picks the numbers, anyway? Somebody doesn't like me around here. Is that what it is, Joey?"

Joey answers, "Everyone likes you. They were waiting for the special day to give you all the money when you play your number, and you didn't play it. You know you're our favorite customer. What number you want today? Since my number came out yesterday, it might not be out for a while yet. You never know. Give me some money, and I'll put it in."

Joey is the neighborhood bookie, who works for his father's illegal family business. Joey always dreams of making it into the big bucks, if only he could place the right bet on something.

Joey goes across the street to the next corner to his friends to discuss politics with Bob, the mayor's son. Joey helped Bob to become the junior class president by using strong-arm tactics and intimidating the students into voting for Bob while Bob paid the rest of them with money or gifts. "Hey, Bob, I heard that we're getting different students this year to add some color to the school. I'll bet you two to one that this school busing thing will be stopped before school opens."

"You're on, Joey. You always were a loser."

They both laugh as Joey writes Bob's name in his numbers book. "Yeah, I'm glad this is my last year, Joey. And If I can spend it as student president, it will look good when I run for councilman-at-large next year. As councilman-at-large, I pledge to fight big business and organized crime, cut taxes, put criminals behind bars, and—"

Joey cuts off his monologue and states, "When you decide to run, let me know so that I can donate to your campaign fund."

They both laugh. While they are laughing, their friends drive up in a convertible car, and then they all go for a ride.

Mayor Patrick Sidel discusses a contingency plan for the antibusing protesters with some members of the council and the police chief. The mayor and the citizens are informed about all of Central High's rejects coming to their school and are against the busing. But the chief of police accepts the busing because this gives him the opportunity to gain recognition for using effective measures for crowd control, which he is proficient in. He imagines the television cameras taping this first-time event since there is so much interest in this issue. Other cities rioted in the past when busing was implemented. The mayor informs the police chief that members of the council have requested the National Guard to be on standby just in case. The mayor tells all assembled that he is up for reelection, and this is the wrong year for busing.

"If I refuse the court order, I could be jailed or fined, and the city could lose federal money. My name would go down in history as anticolored, black, African, Negro . . . you name it. I could never run for governor. I can't have that."

One of the councilmen tells the mayor, "My term expires next year. Leave the governorship for me. You just get on television tonight and tell the world that you're antibusing, and you don't want them peoples at your school. After you say that, I'll run for the governorship, and you can continue as mayor if you're not impeached," the councilman says sarcastically.

The next day, Tony is awakened by his German shepherd, Magnum, again by the usual face licks. Tony sits on the side of his bed and stares at the photo of his brothers that's in front of him. He picks up the picture frame from the table and thinks about his oldest brother, John, in the photo, who overdosed on horse, or, as it's known on the streets, heroin. He remembers watching him sitting on the grass, leaning up against a tree in Faircrest Park. His brother John talked about how good it felt being high on heroin. John added that dope was not for kids because it was a man's high and he wouldn't understand. John told him that it was the only thing that he could achieve in life that made him feel good because he had tried just about everything else. Tony gave John his opinion on achievement and stated that heroin was for losers and that a loser would try any drug to make him feel as if he had achieved something in life.

"Drugs is only a temporary achievement that makes you feel good. Getting that education and accomplishing goals for a better life will last for a lifetime. These drugs will lift your mind up high, but in reality, you're still down in the same position. It's not being down in life but staying down in life that makes you a loser."

John told him, "Yeah, well, after today, I'm going to get right and leave dope alone." With these slurred words, he closed his eyes and died.

Tony's eyes are wet again after reflecting back once more on his brother's senseless death. Before he lets the dog outside, Tony tells the dog to start licking his brother Ace.

"Now that he's home, Ace could let you out in the morning," he mumbled as he slowly walked out of his bedroom.

West Winsor High School is officially open for staff members only on Monday. West Winsor staff members, teachers, janitors, security guards, and student counselors are all getting acquainted with one another. This school year is a very important one for the school mainly because of the mandatory school busing. The former school principal, Mr. King, has resigned in protest over school busing rather than accept African American students at his school under his administration. All the staff members consult with one another, trying to find ways to deal with the new students at West Winsor High. There are only a few new African American employees at the school. One employee named George Wilson works as a custodian. George is starting to receive special treatment and extraordinary attention from the staff. They're practicing how to talk to blacks, coloreds, Negroes, or African Americans for the first time in general conversation, not knowing what they are calling themselves this year. They know they will have to confront such students' parents during the upcoming PTA meeting. So now George (which is what he has been called for the last three years) is being called Mr. Wilson, as if he just changed from a boy to a man at the age of fifty-five. Mr. or Mrs. is how all the staff members have decided to address one another professionally in order for the students to respect them. The staff agreed to set the example first, they thought.

CHAPTER 2

On Monday, the mayor of West Winsor Township holds a meeting with the city council. He wants to find ways to avoid a riot on Wednesday when the court-ordered school busing goes into effect. Mayor Patrick Sidel is feeling a little apprehensive about appointing a woman principal for the school, not knowing if she could handle the pressure and the responsibility this school year. On Wednesday morning, prior to the start of the school year for students, the police, a TV crew, and some protesters begin to gather in front of West Winsor High. The police chief informs the police force that the safety of the bused students is top priority. He also tells them that his wits will keep them from losing control of the situation. As Ace and Tony eat breakfast, their mom tells Ace about the situation that they're about to face.

"Now you know that you're not wanted at West Winsor High, and you're not wanted at Central High. The only institution that would take you in without a fight today is a hospital or a prison. Getting into where you're not wanted is going to be hard. But you're going to have to ingratiate yourself."

Ace tells her, "I don't have no love for those who's not feeling me."

His mom shakes her head and says, "All I'm telling you is to use your brain, that's all."

He took a deep breath, then stated, "All right, Mom, I'll use my brains." That same morning at West Winsor High School, half of the town residents have decided to challenge the mandatory busing court order. The protesters are vehemently against the rejects coming to their city for an education. As the protesters' numbers grow, the small police force begins to worry.

One confused and irritated cop asks the chief, "Are the state police and the National Guard coming soon? The protesters are getting agitated out here."

The chief looks at the officer and smiles. "Don't worry about them. Before the buses get here, I'll have everything under control."

Everybody that is somebody is at the school this early morning. The TV crew is interviewing anyone who is willing to talk. The chief gets a call on the radio that the buses are ten minutes away, so he walks over to the protest organizers and talks to the leader. He is relying on outwitting them to prevent violence. He talks to Bill, who is the head organizer and the community leader who organized this antibusing protest. Bill is also an ex-military commander for the US Army and is ready to battle any probusing supporter, even the police.

The chief walks over to Bill and shakes his hand as he tells him, "Hey, Bill, you sure know how to gather people for a nice welcome party."

Bill angrily tells the chief, "Welcome party? Well, the party hasn't started yet. We're going to show the world how we feel about busing, and it's not going to be nothing nice."

"Now, Bill, every other city in this great country of ours, from the East Coast to the West, rioted to stop school busing, and people got hurt. Cops got hurt, parents got hurt, children got hurt, even cats and dogs got hurt trying to avoid the scuffle. Now my men don't mind swinging their sticks, and I know that the protesters don't mind swinging theirs."

Bill replies, "Yeah, and we're going to do some swinging too!"

"Listen, Bill, the court system doesn't mind us swinging at each other because it doesn't care about us. All it cares about are the laws being forced. You know what happens in all the other cities. If the police can't handle it, they call in the National Guard. If the Guard can't handle it, they'll call the army. You know that. These TV crew members don't care about us either. They've been here all night and here this morning, telling the world about the school's biggest riot. And the one crew member that gets the best camera shot get the Cameraman of the Year Award and paid vacation at our expense. All of the other cities that rioted now have busing, so it's going to happen regardless if we want it or not."

Bill wants to know where the chief's heart and mind is concerning this hostile situation. "Well, Chief, do you like busing?"

"To tell you the truth," the chief begins after removing his hat to wipe his forehead with his handkerchief, "I don't like the fact that someone has to be forced to go somewhere else to get educated, but the law says otherwise. So if we're going to fight, let's fight for something that's ours. This school belongs to the system, and the system can do whatever it wants with it. That's like me trying to tell you how to run your home. Would that be right? Let's give this busing thing a year and see how it works.

If it doesn't, then maybe they'll send the kids somewhere else."

"Chief, we're not going to make this thing work today. Don't you see how big this crowd has gotten? And you have very small police force."

The chief decided to take away Bill's confidence in winning this battle, so he tells him, "You see, Bill, some of those protesters are outsiders, troublemakers, and instigators. They're not from around here. Besides, the state police and the National Guard are on standby in riot gear on the outskirts of town, just waiting to come in and bust heads like they've done in other cities. I told them that this town is not a combat zone. That's why they're not over here on this street with us. Bill, just imagine West Winsor Township as the first city in the country peacefully demonstrating against busing and you as the leading organizer. I'll put a good word in for you to my people. Who knows, somewhere down the line, things might open up for you, to get you a seat as a member on the school board. And you don't have to worry about the condition inside or what things the students will be getting because you'll be calling the shots from the board. So let's end this thing, Bill, and run this school from the inside at the school board. You'll have name recognition as a peacemaker and a problem solver. With credentials like that, I see you sitting on the school board as the school board president."

The chief says this with a confident smile on his face. He walks away as the crowd gets larger and louder. Bill turns to the protesters and begins to talk with them. Police officers begin to worry and wonder if the National Guard really is coming. Also, they're curious about what the chief was talking about.

The chief tells them, "Well, I told him, instead of fighting us, we should have a welcoming party for the new students."

One cop responds, "Why'd you tell him that as much as he hates those people? Now I know we're going to have to fight, and somebody's going to get hurt out here." He says this with a doomsday look on his face.

"Hey, rookie! Don't you have faith in your chief? Trust me. I think I outwitted him."

The TV crews from each station swarm around the chief. One of them asks, "Where's the National Guard and the state police and the—"

Interrupting him, the chief shouts back, "Hold it, hold it, hold it. Now those people were not invited. This is a welcoming party, not a riot. The only reason why there is no cake, doughnuts, and cookies with milk for the kids is because you guys are here, and if you started to eat and drink, there wouldn't be enough for the kids. Besides, you weren't invited either."

"How can you say it's a welcoming party with this angry mob?" the reporter asks.

"The only reason why they're angry is that you guys are here asking stupid questions. If you would've let me know that you were coming, I would've saved a place for you to stand at, instead of you roaming around the streets and sidewalks getting in everybody's way."

The buses begin to roll up the street; the TV crew rushes away from the chief and into the streets before the crowd starts. The crowd is quiet as they watch the students exit the buses. The TV crew members are confused and look at the crowd as they begin to mumble with one another. The cops are confused too. The TV crew attempts to enter the school with the students, but the principal, Mrs. Esteves, blocks their efforts and tells them that they are not allowed to enter without a pass. One of the crew members asks, "Where can we get a pass from?"

She says, "From me, but I'm out of invitations to the party." She turns toward the students, "Welcome to West Winsor High School. There's milk, cookies, and doughnuts inside."

The crew members look perplexed as the chief stands at a distance, shrugs his shoulders, and with a smile, raises both his hands.

While the chief was talking to the TV crew, Bill was telling the protesters that plans were being made to fight this battle in the courts instead of the streets, as the chief suggested. The protesters reluctantly agreed, trusting Bill and his decision. The chief knew Principal Esteves when she worked as a teacher at another school. He knows that her favorite words of greetings to her students, which are "getting milk and cookies," is her symbolic phrase for education. The students are now bewildered, but excited. Everyone in the school is cautious about what to say to one another and curious about how the day will go with all the attention focused on the school.

Nothing unusual happens during school hours, but after school, reporters swamp everyone they can, asking questions about their feelings on school integration and the welcoming party inside.

Joey introduces himself to Ace and Bayshawn as they stand in front of their school bus that's about to depart. Joey is the numbers bookie throughout his neighborhood and school. He stays on the grind making money for his father, who controls all illegal gambling in central New Jersey. Joey tells Ace that if he needed anything in life, except money, just ask.

Joey states, "I'm a businessman, and this is my last year to do business here. As a senior, I'm going out with a bang."

In response, Ace says, "Yeah, this is our first and last year, and it's already a bang."

They stared at each other until Joey says, "I'll see you around!"

As Ace and Bayshawn enter the bus, Joey's friends walk over to Joey to ask what the conversation with Ace was about. On the way home, Bayshawn asks Ace, "So, Ace, what do you think about that school?"

As Ace reflects on what he saw at the school, he tells him, "Something is missing at that school. I don't know what it is, but something is missing, you feel me?"

The presumptive senior class president, Bob, talks to his father, who is the township's mayor, by phone for five minutes. He asks his father, Patrick Sidel, to talk to the school board president to allocate more funds for the schools senior class. At the age of eighteen, Bob is the youngest member and the only student on the school board. With this additional money, the class president could schedule more school trips. "We could all have the best year at West Winsor High by going on class trips and sponsoring different events as well as having the best prom night and dances the school has ever had."

"Hey! Not a bad idea for my son since he's in charge. I'll call the board president and propose $50,000 out of the budget just for the senior class. I'll talk to you later, son."

As the mayor begins to dial, he says, "Howard will push it through. He owes me a favor."

After Bob's father concludes the allocation of funds with Howard, he says to him, "Hey! Don't tell Mrs. Esteves. Let me tell her as soon as the money is available."

"Sure, Mr. Mayor. You have my word," Howard replies.

The bright yellow bus stops in front of Central High. Ace and Bayshawn egress from the bus and holler at some of their friends about West Winsor High. One of their friends tells them that they're changing colors and their voices are changing too.

"I bet y'all don't even get high no more neither."

Bayshawn states, "Yeah, we're getting high. We're getting a high school diploma. That's what counts."

They all laugh and start walking home. While walking, Ace hits his boy Isaiah on his arm and asks, "What do you know about that shorty?"

"Oh, that's Fran'Sheila."

"Yeah! That's her name. My brother told me about her. Who's she with?"

"Ace, nobody's trying to be with that. Let's go and smack her."

"What's up with that? Why smack her?"

"Ace, you've been away too long. The girl is a nobody. She ain't trying to let nobody holla at her. James punched her last week. You ain't hear about it?"

"Naw. What she do to him?"

"She didn't want to kiss him, and she acts like we're ignorant or something."

Ace stops walking and looks at Isaiah, then shakes his head in disbelief. He knows it's because of their immature attitude toward her that makes Fran'Sheila ignore them.

Joey, the numbers bookie, is at Bob's house, asking Bob to endorse him as the school treasurer.

"Brad is running for the treasurer, Bill is running for the secretary, and I'm running for class president."

"Yeah, we know that idiot. Endorse me as the treasurer so that we can get things done this year."

Bob perceives that if Joey is in charge of the money, Joey will have other plans for it. Plus, Joey is the only student Bob has no control over. The $50,000 his father allocated to the class fund was approved.

Bob tells him, "We got things done last year."

"Like what?"

"Well, things! Besides, we already have a bet, which means all I want from you is for you to pay me when I become class president."

Joey blows off steam and says as he points his finger at Bob, "Listen, if you don't endorse me for treasurer, I'll find someone to run against you and win this year. I'm trying to make this thing work for us. I'm the main one who helped put you in position to be class president."

Bob tells Joey, "And I paid you well for that. Don't take this personally, it's all politics. I have everyone paid off, and my influence is very strong. If I'm opposed, everyone that opposes me will suffer for their actions."

Joey stares at Bob, takes a deep breath, takes one step toward Bob, then stops, takes one step back, turns, then walks toward his car, gets in, and speeds away.

Joey finds himself in an unusual predicament. After all the intimidating tactics he used against Bob's potential challengers at school, now he has to find someone to run against Bob, whom he was protecting. While at home, Ace and his brother are discussing school and the consequences of not learning.

"What was up with school today, Tony?"

"I hate those that's there faking it, acting like they're in school for an education. Some of them ain't even trying to learn nothing. School is just a social club for them. I'm not trying to be a part of that. I can't wait until I get out. I think the students should get paid for going, just in case we graduate and can't get a job. I feel as though I'm wasting my time with school."

"But, T, school ain't nothing but an institution for learning, and all that you're learning is a system for standards. That's why they give you a test every so often. Waking up, getting to school on time, performing, and dealing with your classmates and teachers teaches you how to deal with people. These are the things that you must practice with, so when you get a job, that's what you'll have to deal with. So get yourself in good with the people, and deal with the nonsense, but don't get involved in it. Just be aware of it."

Tony tells Ace, "I don't want to be around the nonsense, but I can't seem to avoid it."

"So, T, try not to let it interfere with your work because some people hate to see you make it."

"I can make it on the streets, Ace."

"I know you can, Tony, and I feel what you're saying too. But the streets have no dignity, no values, no respect, and no discipline. And the streets do have a profound effect on your morals too. The only reason why you're not with the crowd is because you've disciplined yourself. Most youngsters your age don't have composure and don't know how to say no when it comes to pleasing the crowd. You see how the crowd runs. Everybody placates to the crowd just to please them. Some in that crowd will run their lives straight to a grave site or prison."

"But what about in prison? Is there a crowd in prison?" Tony asks to get a little knowledge about prison life.

Ace tells him, "Everything that's negative on the streets is in prison. There's no difference."

"How's that Ace?" Tony asks with much curiosity.

"Because everything that is in prison came from out here. The people, laws, material things, the games, drugs, prostitution, homemade wine, all of that you'll see in prison."

"It's like that?" Tony asks.

"Yeah, and if you're not up on it, you're lost. So stay up on the streets because there is knowledge on the streets, but going to school is your way off the streets. School is just a way to discipline yourself for the real world when you're on your own. And the only way to get out of school the right way is for you to go through it the right way."

Isaiah knocks on the door, then walks in.

"Ace, what's good? I heard you called."

"Yeah. I need to go shopping to look like I'm wearing something."

"You do need a new look," Isaiah said as he throws a playful punch at Ace, hitting him in the chest. "You're still soft," he tells Ace while hitting him again, then grabbing Ace in a headlock, until Ace's mom walks in with a broom to break them up.

"Y'all take that out of my house." Ace's mom frowns at the boys. "You should pick on somebody your size."

Isaiah and Ace looks at each other and leave the house.

A short time later, Mrs. Wynn, the boys' basketball coach, tells her husband about their game as he sits down beside her in their den.

"I can get the game added to the schedule, so my guys will be playing your girls for our first game."

"That's good," he said. "It will be your first game and your first loss. And another acknowledgement that when you go against me and my girls, you will always lose."

"Maybe, but just remember, my loss will also be my gain. Because I will never make the same mistake twice."

Her husband made the announcement. "I'm going to advertise this throughout the state of New Jersey. I'll show the world that a good girls' team with a master teacher as a coach could beat a boys' team with a rookie coach. Because if there's a will, there's a way," he says, feeling proud of himself.

After leaving the house, Ace and Isaiah get a ride on the back of a friend's pickup truck on their way to the store. As they ride by people, they shout out to some of their friends. The truck stops at a traffic light, and two more dudes from the hood join them on the truck. While at another traffic light, Sun (his nickname because his complexion is very dark) sees the neighborhood girl whom Ace is feeling, named Fran'Sheila Smith, across the street coming toward them. As they pass her, Sun throws a plastic bottle of soda at her, barely missing her leg. She turns and looks at Ace; they stare at each other while the truck is still moving. Fran'Sheila has a surprised look on her face because she didn't think Ace would be with a crowd like that.

"She thought I did it," Ace tells his boys.

"So what? Tell her you did it. In fact, tell her I did it. It don't mean nothing." Sun told him.

"Yo, you ought to stop that. It don't make no sense for you to be hating on her like that."

"It makes sense to me. And I don't need you to be telling me what I should be doing, you understand?"

"Somebody needs to be telling you how to act. You act like a kid," Ace tells him.

"Well, I could prove that I'm a man to punks like you."

They grab each other and start to tussle while the truck is moving. The driver pulls over, helps break up the tussling match, then tells Sun to walk.

"You must have forgotten who I was, Ace."

"You was soft before, and you're still soft, Sun. All you do is pick on girls, yo."

"You're a girl, Ace. So it ain't no difference. While you were in prison, you was somebody's girl, and now you trying to be a man."

Ace rushes toward Sun as he tells him, "I don't punch like a girl."

Isaiah grabs him, and the driver steps between them and pushes Sun and tells him, "I tried to be nice and give you a ride and you're acting like this. You ain't riding no more."

Sun tells him, "It's like that? It's all good. Ace, I'll run into you again."

"Yeah, and when you do, express yourself with your hands. We ain't gotta talk, Sun."

"All right, I'll do that."

The truck pulls off, leaving Sun and his friend behind.

Joey is in a deli talking to some friends, trying to encourage them to run for student president. Joey tells them, "We need some new blood, someone versatile with new ideas."

"What difference will it make? It's just going to be another boring school year."

"No it's not," Joey tells them. "We could make things happen this school year."

"Who's going to beat Bob? You know he paid off just about everybody. How do you think I got this watch?"

"So if I find someone to run against him, would you back me?"

"Sure, Joey, we'll back you. Who you going to get? Hey! Why don't you try those black aliens we just got."

Joey smiles as he thought about Ace. "So I got your word, uh?"

"Sure, you got our word."

The next day, Ace, Isaiah, and some other friends walk toward Central High School to be transported to West Winsor High School via a bright yellow bus. Ace sees Fran'Sheila walking by herself ahead of them. The neighborhood bully, Sun, is across the street and simultaneously sees her too, but he doesn't see Ace in the crowd. Sun wants to be the first to punch Fran'Sheila, and hopefully, she'll go back home. This is the way he instills fear in the neighborhood. Sun walks across the street toward Fran'Sheila and stops her from walking by grabbing Fran'Sheila's hair with his left hand and gets ready to punch her with his right. As he attempts his first punch, Ace grabs Sun by the arm, turns Sun toward him, and punches Sun in the head, knocking him unconscious. The smiles are removed from everybody's faces and replaced with shocked expressions because no one had ever taken up for Fran'Sheila before. Ace asks her if she is all right. After she responds yes, he tells his friends to walk ahead and he'll catch up with them later. They all agree and walk ahead.

While walking, Ace and Fran'Sheila become well acquainted with each other. He tells Fran'Sheila that she doesn't have to worry about nobody else harassing her anymore because everyone now knows that she is his friend. Before they reach school, everybody seems to know about what happened. So now a lot of Ace's friends are greeting Fran'Sheila with respect. Ace kisses her on the cheek and enters the bus, then tells her to wait for him here after school. She agrees to that.

CHAPTER 3

As the bright yellow bus stops in front of West Winsor High School, Joey looks for Ace to come off the bus. While waiting, one of Joey's friends asks, "So, Joey, who are you endorsing for class president? Who's the mystery man? Who's the guy that's going to outsmart and outpay Bob? Is it you, Joey, huh? Who is he? Or is it a she? Or what is it? Talk to me, Joey."

Joey smiles and tells him, "I'll let you know in the near future."

After saying this, he walks over to Ace, shakes his hand, and tells him that he is endorsing him for senior class president. He then asks Ace if he will accept.

"Why me?" Ace asks with a surprised and perplexed look. "I don't even know these people. Plus I'm an outsider in all respects."

"See, that's the point. We need a new president for a new start. We've accomplished nothing with this guy Bob last year as junior class president. His father is the mayor, so Bob thinks that he is above everyone else. The student president chooses where we go on field trips. I'm tired of going to the opera shows, the ice hockey games, and the ballet dances. For our last year, we need to make this our best year. All of my friends said that they wouldn't run against Bob. They said if I found someone to run against him, they would support me and back my candidate."

Ace asks curiously, "So why don't you run against him?"

"Because," Joey says after taking a deep breath, "because I'm running for the job of student treasurer. But, Ace, you'll be in charge of the finances."

They stare at each other. Then Ace tells him after thinking about it for a few, "I'll let you know something by the end of the day. Meet me here at three o'clock."

"Sure, Ace. Thanks for your time."

As Joey walks away, Bayshawn walks over to Ace and asks, "What did he want? Ain't that the dude who said if you need anything, just come see him?"

"That's him," Ace responds.

"Well, we don't need him or anything he has to give. We can hold our own at this school. You feel me?"

"You already know, but hear me on this. Joey wants me to run for class president so that I can choose our school trips, control the class money, and bring some life into this school."

"Word, I'll vote for you if you run. We could make some changes around here. I'll be your vice president, and when they assassinate you, I'll be in charge."

They laugh at the idea while walking up the steps to the school. The mayor calls the school principal, Mrs. Esteves, on the phone to ask about the school's activity that morning before school starts.

"Hey, Mrs. Boss Lady, how's it going at the big house?"

"Mr. Mayor, it's a surprise to hear from you this morning."

"Why is it a surprise to hear from me?"

"Because you said you would only call me if there was a problem."

"Well, Mrs. Esteves, there is a problem. There're a lot of complaints about the school, and everybody is asking me questions that I have no answers to. When I refer them to you, they tell me that you don't want to talk."

"Oh, that's nonsense, Patrick. I talk. I tell them that everything is okay and no further comment."

"Yes, but they want answers, and you're not explicit enough."

"Well, I'm not going to write them a book. Besides, if there's a problem, I'll tell you first."

"Mrs. Esteves, you haven't told me anything yet."

"That's because there's no problem yet, Mr. Mayor."

"How's the school busing going?"

"Oh, it's just fine."

"Why was the basketball coach fired?"

"Because of incompetence," she replies with no regrets.

"Why do the male teachers have to open the doors for the female employees?"

"That's part of being a man," she responds with conviction.

"Why did you change the staff meeting from Wednesday to Friday?"

"So that we could have a fresh start on Monday, Mr. Mayor."

"Why are you building a woman's staff room?"

"Oh, that," she says as if she has forgotten. "Well, boys will be boys!"

"You know that you're the number one enemy at the school," the mayor tells her.

"Now, who would want to hate me?"

"Well, that's not important. Listen, I'm sending an extra $50,000 down for the senior class. Please don't interfere with it. It's for the class, okay?"

"Sure, Pat. The class president is in charge."

"Hey!" the mayor said as if he almost forgot. "Tell Coach Wynn to start my son, Bob, every game during the regular season, and I'll see to it that she gets that coaching job at Rutgers University next year. That's my promise."

During that morning, while school is in session, Fran'Sheila finds Ace's class and asks the teacher if he can be excused. Ace is surprised and wondering what this visit is all about.

"What's good, lady?"

She kisses him on the cheek and says, "Hi. I just wanted to thank you for this morning and show you that I really appreciate what you've done for me."

"Yeah? But I asked you to meet me at the school this afternoon. You didn't have to come here to do this."

"You're right. But I wanted to."

"How did you get here?"

"My girlfriend drove me here."

"I have to go back inside. Meet me at the school at three thirty, okay?"

"Sure, Ace."

He kisses her cheek and returns to class. When Ace enters the class, the bell rings. The teacher tells Ace, who has picked up his books and is heading for the door, "Young man, I don't allow my classes to be interrupted unless it's urgent."

"I apologize, Mr. Ginn, but anytime someone comes for me in the middle of class, it is urgent."

"What was so urgent about that interruption?"

"Oh, that was personal."

Ace leaves the class and goes to the gym for his next class. At gym, the gym teachers are still asking the students if there were any more doctors' excuses because gym class will officially open tomorrow. The teachers are finding out if all the students who will be participating have assigned lockers. The whole gym is open to the students. Some are on the floor shooting baskets; a number of them are just sitting around talking. Bayshawn is on the court with his friends who were also transferred from Central High, reminiscing about how they took the state basket championship last season. Bob, who is West Winsor High's basketball captain, is listening with his friends while Bayshawn is on the court shooting the ball. Bayshawn says while smiling, "I heard that this school ain't got no ballplayers."

After Joey takes a jump shot on the court, Joey looks at Bob, the captain, and says out loud, "I heard this school had a good playing captain." Bayshawn shouted back, "I heard that his ball game is weak."

Ace walks on the court with his gym clothes on and shakes hands with his friends while Bayshawn is still talking.

"Tell 'em, Ace. This school ain't got no ballplayers, does it?"

Bob gets up from the bench, feeling disrespected by his former rivals, and tells Bayshawn, "Your game is weak too. That's why you're here now. You know your coach didn't want you on his team because your ball game is weak."

Bayshawn shouts back, "I was forced to leave the school. That's why I'm here. Keep it real when you talk about me."

Bob walks onto the court and says to Bayshawn, "They lied to you, and that's the excuse you use. You don't really got no ball game, do you? If you do, put your money in your hand to back your words up. So what do you want to do?"

Joey interrupts the exchange and says, "I'll clear the court and hold the money for each team. Bob, you get five players, and, Bayshawn, you get your five."

Ace tells them, "Fifty dollars a man, and I'll get ours."

He runs to his locker as Bob borrows money from his friends that are sitting on the bleachers. Joey asks all students that are not playing to please leave the court. Then Joey pays a guy to keep the score on the time clock. When all the players are on the court, the grudge match begins. As the game is being played, the school's basketball coach, Mrs. Wynn, is in her office on the phone. As each minute goes by, some of the students interrupt her and ask Mrs. Wynn to come out to observe the game. Each time her door opens, the noise from the gym gets louder from the excitement of the game. She is indignant because the order for gym supplies is inadequate. Also she is upset because she is constantly being interrupted by the students, especially one named Susan. Susan is Mrs. Wynn's basketball talent scout. Susan opens the door to ask Mrs. Wynn to come out to the gym to look at the school's potential basketball team. But the coach is still upset about the order and is trying to rectify it over the phone before the day is over so that the order can arrive in time for gym classes tomorrow.

"I think you should hang up the phone and see this," Susan says.

Mrs. Wynn puts the man on hold, then angrily gets up to see what all the commotion is all about. When she enters the gym, one of West Winsor's team players shoots a jump shot on Squib, a five-foot-seven guard who jumps almost to the top of the backboard. Squib got his nickname because of his height. Squib throws the jump shot into the crowd as he blocks it.

"Was he trying to shoot that on me, huh? Was he trying to shoot that? Or was that a pass, Bayshawn?" Squib asks that with all seriousness, as if it was impossible for someone to shoot on him and make a shot.

"He was trying to shoot. I saw him, Squib," Bayshawn tells him while laughing.

"He better act like he know next time."

Bob inbounds the ball to one of his teammates. West Winsor's guard dribbles the ball while Squib is playing him. He fakes Squib to the left, then goes to the right, shoots the ball, hitting all net.

He asked his teammates, "Was someone playing me, huh? Was there someone on me, or was they playing a zone?"

"Yeah, I was on you. You only made one."

"No, no, no. That's two points! Two! I shook you so hard, now you can't even add right. I thought you went to get some water or something. Maybe y'all should be playing a zone."

Bayshawn gives Squib an alley-oop pass; Squib catches it on the side of the rim and dunks it in backward. The crowd is surprised that this five-foot-seven student could jump that high.

Ace tells him, "Cut that out, yo. They don't know nothing about that." Another West Winsor player brings the ball up the court and has it stolen. Ace is running up the court on the wing, or the edge of the floor, when he receives the ball. He runs to the basket, cuffs the ball on his right arm while he is rocking it, glides to the basket, and slam-dunks the ball. The crowd reacts with euphoria.

West Winsor High's teammates are not used to the "run and gun" game, and they are confused because they are being pressured full court. The street game is much different from the basic, fundamental game they're used to playing. Mrs. Wynn watches one more play as Ace grabs the ball and shakes his man, dribbles the ball, and does a 360 jump shot that hits all net. The crowd stands on their feet in shock. Mrs. Wynn looks at Susan, then looks at the crowd and remembers the incorrect equipment order. She becomes more disgusted as she walks back to her office. She walks inside, slams the door, sits in her chair, gets back up, locks the door to avoid any more interruptions, and goes back to her chair. After all this, she finds that there is no one on the other end of the phone line she had placed on hold. So she calls the man back to ask about her team's basketball uniforms. The man tells her the school's coach said there is no team this season, so he canceled the new uniforms. He asks if the school has a coach and starts laughing.

"Yes, the school has a coach. I'm the new coach," she snapped back at him. As the man continues to laugh, she tells him, "And you want something else to laugh at? We're going to win all of our games because . . ." She pauses and thinks about the players she just saw. Mrs. Wynn throws the phone on the desk and runs to the door. She pulls the doorknob, forgetting that she put the lock on the door, and jerks the knob off. She tries to twist the cylinder with her fingers, then tries to put the knob back on. The cylinder falls out through the other side because of her banging on the knob. Mrs. Wynn becomes so frustrated that she bangs on the door with her fist, but the crowd is too loud for anyone to hear her. So she picks up a chair and throws it through the stained glass window. When some of the students look to see what happened, she tells one of them to get the knob and put it in the door to let her out. After the student opens the door, Mrs. Wynn goes to Susan and tells her to get the players' names. As Ace, Bayshawn, Isaiah, and Squib run by, Susan hollers out to them with a pen and a pad in her hands, "Hey, what's your name?" But nobody responds. So Mrs. Wynn joins her in shouting, "Hey, what are your names?"

The time expires on the clock. The score is a blowout. While Joey still has the money in his hand, he notices a teacher pointing at him to the security guard. This teacher knows that Joey is a gambler and watched him take money from the players. As the guard comes toward them with the teacher, Joey tells the players not to tell them their names.

"They think we're gambling. Let's go. Don't tell them your names. Don't say nothing," Joey tells Ace's team as they run toward the locker room door.

The security guard, the teacher, Susan, and Mrs. Wynn ask Ace, Bayshawn, Isaiah, and Squib their names again and again. Nobody responds.

"Did you get their names, Susan?" Mrs. Wynn asks.

"No, they didn't answer me."

"Why didn't you grab one of them? You let them get away?"

"I tried, Mrs. Wynn, but . . ."

"You should have tripped one of them or something, Susan."

Susan is at a loss for words as the coach walks away disgusted again. After Bayshawn and Ace get dressed, they are escorted with Joey to the principal's office. The teacher and the security guard are in the office, talking with the principal, Mrs. Esteves, about the gambling and the betting that they witnessed. Regardless of what they saw Joey do, they are determined to get Ace and Bayshawn kicked out of school for gambling.

"You see, they should be expelled from school and fined to set an example for all of the students," the teacher tells Mrs. Esteves. "Next it will be drugs and who knows what else. This used to be a decent school until those people came here with their illegal activities. They even got this good kid Joey involved in this . . . this . . . this mess here."

"Yeah! And they ran out of the gym and down to the locker room. If they had their street clothes on, they would've run out of school," the guard said. "I've never had to run after any student before, and I hope this is the last time after you get rid of them."

The principal's eyes got wider as she looks at them, surprised. "Well, gentlemen, let's ask the boys to come in so that we can have their confession."

The guard lets them into the office. The boys sit down, stare at each other, then look at the principal. She asks them, "Do you know why you're here?"

Ace tells her, "Yes, for having money."

The teacher tells him, "You're here for gambling. That's not only a school violation but also a city, county, state, and federal violation as well. I don't know if they allow that in the school you came from, but we don't allow it here."

The principal interrupts, "Excuse me. I'll give the statements and ask the questions. Let's hear their side of the story." Mrs. Esteves asks the boys, "Whose money is this?"

"It's mine," Ace told her.

"Did you win this from gambling, playing basketball?"

"No," Ace responded.

"Did you bring it from home?"

"Yes," Ace says as if it was a crime for him to have money.

"Did you always have it on you?"

"No," Ace responded.

"When didn't you have it on you?"

"I was playing basketball in the gym, and I didn't want to leave it in my locker, so I asked Joey to hold it for me. When the game was over, he gave it back to me."

Mrs. Esteves asked, "So why did you run when these two gentlemen called you?"

"They were running after us, and somebody said run. I didn't know what was going on, so I ran with the rest of the students down to the locker room and got dressed."

"Did anyone ask you where you got the money from?"

"Nobody asked that. They took it and brought us here. I thought it was against the school's policies to have money in this school, the way these two grabbed me."

"Come on. Do you expect her to believe that lie? If you weren't gambling, you wouldn't have run." After the teacher tells Ace this, he looks at Bayshawn and asks him, "What did you say your name was?"

"My name is Bayshawn."

"Well, Mr. Bay, Tell us why you ran."

"It's Bayshawn, idiot. My name is Bayshawn. Get my name right and act like you know!"

The teacher, now shocked by his response, shouts at Mrs. Esteves, "Did you hear what he called me? Did you hear that? They don't have any respect for us or anyone else." He looks at the security officer and asks him, "Did you hear him?" This teacher tells the principal, "I demand that they be expelled from this school immediately. I don't have to take insults from any student. I give respect to everyone, now I'm getting insulted by these . . . these—"

The principal interrupts him and says, "Let me handle this, all right? I'm trying to get an understanding of this situation."

Mrs. Esteves has no reason to suspend or expel any of the boys, so she tells them, "Boys, if you are running, walking, or doing anything else and a staff member asks you to come to them, please give them your undivided attention like you're doing now. Would that be a problem?"

Each of the boys says that they don't have a problem with that and that they would comply. When the principal dismisses them from her office, the teacher and the guard are in disbelief.

"You're not going to let them get away with this, are you? How could you just let them walk out of here like that?" the teacher asks.

"Gentlemen, it's been a long day. Please leave the door open after you leave, and have a nice day," she says this with a smile on her face while sitting in her chair.

In the hall, after leaving the principal's office, Ace tells Joey and Bayshawn, "Yo, that didn't make any sense, did it? They were really trying to get rid of us, weren't they? I know they're going to be hating on us now because they're vexed."

"Ace, everybody likes you. That's why they're backing you for student president," Joey tells him.

"Ain't nobody backing me up for president."

"Tell him, Bayshawn, everybody's backing him," Joey says.

"I don't know nothing about these people, but I'll back him, and that's all he needs 'cause nobody's real around here."

Joey asks, "Ace, it's the end of the school day. Let me know something so we can get this candidacy started."

They stop walking and stare at Ace. Ace takes a deep breath, looks at both of them, and then tells them, "Look,

I'm no politician. All I want to do is get in school, go through it, and get out of here as quiet as possible."

Bayshawn tells him, "Hey, partner. We're the first ones in here, and we're going to be the first ones out. But while we're here, we need someone to represent our people so that we can set an example for those that come after us. That way, we could let this administration know what our priorities are and how we should be treated, then we won't get harassed. You feel me?"

Joey tells Ace, "Look, you'll have control of the money and how it's spent on dances and school trips. I'll let you know what needs to be done, and then you'll decide if it should be done."

Bayshawn tells both of them, "Yeah, we can do this. We can run this school the way it's supposed to be run. Let's make it happen, Ace. Let's represent our people while we're here."

Ace smiles at them and says, "Gentlemen, I accept your endorsement for senior class president. Let's run this school."

The three of them shake hands and continue to walk. That afternoon at home, Mrs. Wynn tells her husband that she thinks she has a team this season. "All coaches have a team," he says sarcastically. "In fact, a real coach knows that he has a team and knows all of the players that are on the team too. The coach knows the player's ability to play on the court as well. That's all a part of a coach's job. Aren't you glad you have me as a husband who is a coach who can give you this kind of information?"

She looks at him as if to say, "I didn't ask you all of that."

He smiles at her and says, "What do you mean you think you have a team? It's either you do or you don't."

"Well, I saw these kids shooting the ball and making all kinds of shots. They were running up and down the court real fast, blocking shots, and doing lightning passes. It was amazing! But I don't know who they were."

"You saw all of this?"

"Yes, but when I tried to ask them their names, they ran."

"So you should have stopped them."

"I couldn't. They ignored me and kept running."

Her husband, Jim, is confused about her story, so he asks, "Hold it. Hold it. You've got the worst team in the state and ballplayers in your gym playing like that, and you couldn't even get their names? It couldn't have been students from your school! Your students couldn't do that all year."

She tells him, "Well, I'm going to see tomorrow if I can get their names." Jim says to her, as if he has this great idea, "Listen, starting tomorrow, make an announcement that the gym is open for unofficial basketball practice after school. Then, when the students come to play ball, you'll see what kind of talent you have, and just scout from there. How does that sound, hon?"

"Okay, I'll try that and see if it works or not. That way, I could have a start on all the other teams before they begin practice next month. I could be well prepared before the season starts! Hey! Good idea. Thanks." She kisses him on his lips and then hugs him.

He looks her in her eyes and says to her, "Dear, all of the coaches in the nation have been doing that for years. Now, do I still have the first game with your team?"

"Yes!" she says with excitement. "You do get to have the first defeat from my team, but don't take it personally. It's only a game."

That afternoon, Ace and Bayshawn get off the bus at Central High School, where Fran'Sheila said she would be waiting for Ace. After kissing her cheek, Ace tells Bayshawn that he'll holler at him later and puts his arm around Fran'Sheila's waist and begins to walk with her. While waking, Ace tells her, "You know that you'll be getting a lot of attention now, don't you?"

"I've always got attention, Ace. You know that everybody hates me."

"If I hated you, we wouldn't be walking together. I'm feeling you now, but I need to know something about you."

They stop walking and face each other. Ace tells her, "I'm not going to ask all of the things that you like because I know that you have a million likes. So I'm going to ask you what do you dislike in a man or in his ways."

She thinks for a moment and then tells him, "Well, first I have to get to know you. Because what I might not like in you could be your natural way of life. In other words, what I dislike might be a normal way of life to you. So it wouldn't be fair for me to change your natural way of life. That's what makes you who you are. Just treat me the way you think I should be treated, with respect. And I will reciprocate. But if I feel disrespected, I'll let you know."

Ace thinks about what she has said and then tells her, "If we treat each other too good, we might fall in love and live happily ever after."

"Well, Ace, that usually happens to people."

"But love hurts, lady, and I'm afraid of love."

"No, Ace, love doesn't hurt. It's that the one that you love sometimes hurts you. I have no intentions of hurting you. Already you've shown me a token of love by what you've done for me. Maybe I'm going too fast for myself, Ace, but I'm ready to do for us because I'm feeling you."

Ace puts both hands on her waist as he tells her, "I'm feeling you on that, and I'll keep that in mind, lady."

They kiss and continue to walk with a little more understanding about each other. On the way home from school, Bayshawn sees his friends sitting on a porch in the hood. They see him with schoolbooks in his hand and smile as he walks toward them. After shaking their hands, one of them asks Bayshawn, "What's good, and what's up with that school? Y'all gonna be staying there until they run y'all out or what?"

Bayshawn shakes his head and says, "Ace is going to be making a lot of changes at that school because he's going to be the man. And when he's the man—"

His friend interrupts to ask, "Wait, wait, what kind of changes? What do you mean by 'the man'?"

"Listen, yo. Don't interrupt me when I'm trying to explain things, you feel me?"

"I feel you. My bad. I forgot that's not polite." His friends giggle.

"Ace is running for student president," Bayshawn tells them.

One of his friends spits out the beer he just put in his mouth as they laugh at what Bayshawn told them. Bayshawn also tells them that he is backing Ace with his campaign. Finally, one of them says, "Bayshawn, y'all are about fifteen to twenty miles away at another city, at another school trying to run things. Y'all dudes might get killed out there. Hold it. I'll give you my gun 'cause if you gonna be running things, then you might as well protect yourself the right way."

"I don't need a gun. All we need is our brains. With that, we'll get the job done."

The guy who spit the beer out tells his friends, "I told you these dudes done changed. They're even thinking crazy. Bayshawn, all you and Ace got to do is go to school and, at the end of the school day, leave. That's all."

"Look, I don't need you telling me how to finish school when you quit school at the end of the school year. That don't make any sense."

"Yes, it does. I went to school in the morning and left in the afternoon. I just ain't been back yet. But I'll be back when I'm ready."

Another friend asks, "What makes you think that Ace is going to run the school if he's elected, Bayshawn?"

"Because he got this dude named Joey backing him up. Joey is with them Italian boys that's in the mob, and they be pushing up on people big time. Let me put y'all up on this. See, the student president is in charge of the money for the students, and they already got a big bank account from last year. Once Ace is in charge of the money, if anyone touches him, it's like touching the mob. And those boys ain't no joke."

Another friend asks, "Yeah, Bayshawn, but first he got to get in, right?"

Bayshawn tells him, "We're manipulating that now as we speak. So as far as I'm concerned, he's already in 'cause I'm backing him."

"Oh, word? It sounds like y'all got it going on."

They all shake Bayshawn's hand, then one of them tells him, "When you see Ace, tell him I said to stay strong."

With those words, Bayshawn continues to walk.

Ace enters his house with lipstick on his cheek. His brother Tony sees the lipstick, smiles, and shakes his head. Ace looks at Tony's smile and asks, "What's good? How was school?"

"School was all right. How was school with you?"

Ace smiles and says, "It was interesting."

Tony tells him, "Yeah, I heard. What's this about you punching Sun in the face over some girl?"

"Who told you that?"

"Everybody told me about you. You can't deny it because you still have lipstick on your face."

"Naw, it wasn't like that, T. I just protected the girl, that's all," Ace says while wiping his face with his hand.

"Yeah, then she gave you a kiss on your cheek, right?"

"Well, when you do nice things for girls, nice things happen to you."

"All right, all right," Tony tells him as if to say that he's not trying to hear that. "I heard that you knocked him out. Does this mean that I have to get strapped when I leave the house? 'Cause they say that Sun ain't no punk. And you knocked him out like that. I know that he's swollen by now."

"T, me and Sun had a few words, that's all."

"Naw, that ain't all, Ace. Here you are telling me to use my head and not my fist. Then you go and punch this dude because y'all had some words before over some woman. I knew someday you would get me killed. What I'm supposed to do now?"

"T, ain't nobody trying to kill you over what I did. That was between me and him. You know he's a bully. So when he tries to bully my friend, I had to step to him, that's all."

"I heard you punched him over Fran'Sheila. I didn't know that you were into that. It must be love if you knocked him out."

"It ain't love. You're hearing too much. When it is love, I'll let you know."

"All right, Ace. Then you can tell me what love is all about so that I can go and knock somebody out."

Ace gives him a strange look and walks upstairs. The phone rings. Ace picks up the phone, and it's Joey.

"Hey, dude, I want to get with you to go over your speech for the debate. What about six o'clock this evening?"

"Six will work for me, Joey. Come pick me up. I'll be in front of Central High School."

"Okay, I think I know where it's at. It's across the street from two gas stations, right?"

"You already know, Joey."

"See you at six, Ace." As Joey hangs the phone up, Joey's mom enters the room.

"Joey, the school called and said you were gambling and running with hoodlums and gang members in the gym. Is that true?"

"Ah, Mom. Who told you that?"

"Never mind who told me. I just want you to be careful who you choose as friends and to take care of yourself because I trust you and love you."

Joey kisses her cheek and says, "Thanks, Mom. I'm being careful. But I do have a lot of people that are hating on me. So there are those that would lie on me."

"Just be careful, Joey."

"All right, Mom."

CHAPTER 4

That evening, Sun walks toward Ace's house, looking for revenge. He sees the same dudes Bayshawn has spoken to earlier. When they see him, they begin to whisper to one another. As Sun comes toward them, one of them ask sarcastically, "What's good, Sun? I heard you got burnt today." The guys sitting on the porch start laughing.

"Don't start with me, yo. You can get the same thing he's gonna get when I unlock and unload on him with this nine gun," Sun said this while showing them the nine-millimeter handgun he has tucked in his pants, on his waist.

"I don't know, Sun. Ain't no need for that. I mean, if you're gonna fight the man, fight the man with your hands."

"I am fighting with my hands, except I'll be squeezing, that's all."

Another guy tells him, "How you gonna kill a man over a woman anyway? If you squeeze on him, you're back in jail, partner. You didn't have no win then, and you don't have a win now."

Sun tells him, "I did time before. I'ma handle mine the way I choose to handle it."

The same guy asks Sun, "So now you want to fight by squeezing because you try to punch a girl and you got dropped?"

Sun snaps back, "I fight the way I want to fight. And what do you got to do with this anyway?"

"I'm just trying to save your life. Bayshawn came by here and said that Ace is in the mafia and that he's controlling their money in the school he's in. You know that if you interfere with their money, they're coming after you."

Sun tells him, "Then I'll just take on the mob too."

The other guy shakes his head and tells Sun, "You should just leave the situation alone. You shouldn't have been trying to punch that girl anyway. In fact, you should apologize to her."

"You crazy," Sun snaps back at him.

"All right, Sun. If the mob comes for you, I don't know you, and you don't know me."

"That's fine with me," Sun told him. As he continues to walk, Sun sees Ace's brother Tony on the sidewalk and asks him about Ace. Tony informs him that Ace has gone to the high school to meet somebody. Sun thinks that Ace has gone to meet Fran'Sheila, so he runs to the high school. Sun plans on shooting both of them there.

When he arrives at Central High School, he sees Ace standing in front of the school by himself. Then a black Mercedes Benz pulls up. Joey gets out of the driver's seat, goes around the car, and opens the door for Ace. Joey greets him with all smiles, then shuts the door, gets in the driver's seat, and drives away. Sun is convinced that what he was told about Ace is true, so he walks away puzzled, not knowing that Tony is there standing at a distance with a bat in his hands, watching.

As they rode to discuss their strategy, Joey informs Ace about how he defamed Bob's reputation on Twitter and Facebook and by texting all his contacts from school.

The next day during school, after Ace continued to receive information about his opponent, Bob, Ace is now prepared and confident to face his challenger. Joey is excited too, but he wants to be professional about this debate. The debate is scheduled for 12:00 p.m. The students are to be assembled in the auditorium at this time. Joey plans to be Ace's cheerleader during the debate. Joey told Ace everything he needed to know about Bob and the student class presidency.

About 9:00 a.m., Bob and his friends are in the student study hall talking. Bob, not knowing who is running against him, is discussing with them how important the election is and expressing curiosity about who is going to run against him. Bob thought about what Joey said to him during their last encounter and tells them, "You know what? I think that idiot is going to run against me himself. Everybody knows that he's a crook and a gangster and that his father is in the mob. We have too much money in the account to let him steal it. Hey! That's what I'll say to the students when I get on stage. I'll just get on stage, say what I got to say, and let him defend himself from that while we're in our seats thinking about how to spend the money." They laugh at his idea. While still laughing, there is a knock at the door. Joey and Ace enter.

"Hey, Bob. Good morning, gentlemen," Joey says.

"What do you want, Joey? We were just talking about you," Bob tells him. Then Bob and his friends begin to snicker.

"Hello, Bob. I was thinking about how unfortunate it is for you to not have me for your running mate as student treasure. But the show must go on. I've found an intelligent young man who is a beacon for our school's future and has a keen sense of direction for this school. I feel that he is qualified to beat you in this campaign for student council class president."

Bob asks, "Who is this young man that you found to beat me, Joey?"

Joey turns to Ace and then introduces Ace as Bob's opponent to all that are present. Bob and his friends look perplexed. They look at each other without saying a word, then begin to giggle. The giggle turns to laughter. While laughing, Bob says to Joey, "Is this the best you can do?"

One of Bob's friends falls on one knee while laughing uncontrollably. Ace and Joey look at each other before turning around and walk out of the student lounge.

All morning, Bob and his friends ridicule Joey and the colored kid running against Bob. The whole school is interested in how the debate will turn out. At 12:00 p.m., the auditorium is packed. The questions of the day are, who is Ace? What does he look like? What is he going to say? And can he really beat Bob?

The speaker introduces Bob and Ace to the students. The first candidate to speak is Bob. Bob addresses the students and says, "My fellow students, this is our last year at West Winsor High School. I've been attending this school since the ninth grade, and I might add that I had some fun times here. As student president, I would guarantee that all of you will have a fun time here too. Now I don't know anything about my opponent, and he knows nothing about us or our school. Maybe he wants to make our school the way his former school is, which couldn't have been much—that's why he's here."

Some in the audience begin to laugh. Bob continues, "But if you elect me as president, we could make this our best senior class ever. Thank you."

The students applaud. Next, the speaker introduces Ace to the students. Ace looks at them as if he is disgusted and says, "Good afternoon, students. My name is Ace Sherrod. As you will find out that when it comes to a challenge against all odds, I'm the one who can and will face the challenge and beat it because I'm determined to do what's best and dedicated to doing what's right. In class, I'm studying business academics, money management, and political science. Contrary to what my opponent said about me, I do know a lot about him, and I know that he is the wrong choice for class president. He said that your school trips were boring. I have to add that my opponent is boring. And now he wants to schedule the school trips."

Joey hollers, "Don't let him do it!"

"As president, I'm going to start a program so that every senior gets a half day off from school if they show that they've received a job interview during school hours for Career Day."

Joey hollers again, "Yeah!"

"How are we going to procure employment while we're in class? We need time out of school for job interviews. If we take a day off from school, they'll hold that against us. By the time we graduate, all of the summer jobs will be taken. So we need to be out there on the grind, trying to get a job while the job is still available."

Joey hollers his approval again. As Ace reflects on his encounter with the security guard in the principal's office, he states, "I'm also tired of students being harassed in this school by these security guards in the halls. They always try to rush us to class so they can continue to play their card games while we're in class." Ace states as he turns toward the guard who chased him to the locker room, "They want to chase us through the halls for no reason."

Joey hollers again, and other students join him. Ace continues by saying, "The guards always tell us to keep walking and to pick up the trash that's in the halls. They should be picking up the trash in the halls because some of them are the ones that throw their trash on the floors in the hall." Ace continues to talk with conviction and says, "As student president, I would like to introduce a new class at West Winsor High. I would like to introduce and recommend a criminal justice or pre-criminal justice course. It's unfortunate that most people receive criminal education while they're incarcerated in prison. In other words, they learn about the laws that govern them after they have been arrested. The course I'm recommending would help us to understand our rights as students prior to hiring an attorney and as law-abiding citizens if we're accused of any crime."

The students applaud and whistle. Ace continues, "Law enforcement officials, such as policemen, corrections officers, US marshals, sheriff officers, district attorneys, lawyers, and judges, have all studied criminal justice courses. All of us have the potential to become any of the mentioned occupations. If we decide to take this course in high school, we'll be one step up on the laws and a step ahead of the course. And we'll be a step ahead of students from other schools if we have already studied the subject here, prior to college."

The students applaud again. Ace resumes, "I want West Winsor High to take the lead as being the first in the state, setting an example for the future. The only way to do that is by being innovative and creative. My concepts will take us far into the future while others"—Ace glances at Bob—"continue the same old things"—he says sarcastically—"that will benefit themselves. From the beginning of the school year, the whole world has been watching us, so now is the time to show the world what can be accomplished if we work together. Thank you."

A majority of the students who are in the auditorium gave Ace a standing ovation with smiles of approval. At the end of the school day, Ace won the election. Joey's intimidating tactics convinced many students to vote for Ace and for him as the treasurer.

The unofficial basketball tryout allows Coach Wynn to view the players. The coach, who saw just what she was looking for, has just picked her team before making the announcement for team tryouts for the school's basketball team. The team's captain, Bob, who has lost the election, knows what Ace can do on the court. And he knows that Ace has the potential to be captain. Bob promises the coach that he will make sure the team improves 100 percent if he remains the team's captain.

After his long celebration with his lady, Fran'Sheila, along with Joey and his girl, Ace finally sees himself as a leader. After practice, Joey drives Isaiah, Bayshawn, and Ace home.

Joey tells them, "You know what, fellas, I think that I should be the manager of the basketball team, just to make sure that the team is organized. You see, I know you guys don't like them, and those guys don't like y'all.

You know what I mean? I can be the diplomat between the two groups and make it so that everyone's happy."

Bayshawn asks, "Yeah, Ace, what's up with you and Bob? He still catching feelings, huh? He didn't get elected, and now he's acting like a baby."

"Yeah, and my skin color doesn't help neither," Ace tells them.

After Joey drops them off, he heads for home. While in the hood in Wilbur Section, Joey approaches a traffic light that's red on the corner of East State and Chambers Street. There are four dudes standing on that corner looking at his Mercedes Benz. Joey's music is loud with the sounds of R&B banging off his back window. One of the dudes tells Joey that he's listening to the wrong radio station. He tells him, "You need to stop playing yourself. We're not impressed with your ride or your music. You need to put some twenty-inch rims on that. And put that radio on a rock-and-roll station. You know, that's what you be listening to when you're not in our neighborhood."

Joey turns to different stations on his radio until he finds an acid rock song to placate them. One gentleman says to him, "Yeah, that's it."

The light turns green, and Joey drives two blocks with the widows down while the radio plays loud acid rock music. He stops at another red light when two females pull up beside him and notice him smiling with his head bobbing up and down. The young ladies smile at him and roll down their car window to speak. But when they hear what kind of music he is listening to, they look at each other and frown, shake their heads, and roll the windows back up. When the light turns green, the ladies speed away, and when Joey realizes why, he begins to change the radio stations. Joey hollers out to them to stop as he changes the station, but to no avail. So he gives up as they drive away.

That evening, after Joey dropped Ace off, Ace is on his way to Fran'Sheila's house when a neighborhood thug named Rock approaches him to make a business offer for Ace to sell crack and weed for him. Ace refuses the offer and tells him that he's not trying to go back to jail and that he has a good reputation in the neighborhood.

"Ace, listen. I'm not telling you to lose your reputation in the hood. All I'm asking for you to do is to introduce my products to the students at your school, that's all. You ain't gotta offer nobody in the hood nothing. Besides, you'll be getting mad pay for it anyway. I'll give you half."

"I don't know, Rock. I'm in too many things now already."

"So drop them, Ace. I'm where the money's at."

"I'll think about it, Rock, all right?"

"All right, Ace, get back at me." They shake hands and then walked in opposite directions.

Ace goes to Fran'Sheila's house for the evening. They greet each other with a hug then poke at each other.

"So, Ace, you made the basketball team, huh?"

"I was supposed to make it," Ace said with much confidence.

Fran'Sheila asks, "So does that mean that all of my time with you will be limited because of all your activities?"

"Not really, I'll find time for you, lady. Just don't be too demanding or possessive."

"Ace, if it's my time, then I want what's mine."

Ace responds by saying, "And if it's mine, then I want what's mine too."

"I'll give you yours. Meaning that you will have your freedom, Ace."

"That's what's up, lady. Because you know I love my freedom."

She looks at Ace with a smirk on her face and says, "So, Ace, if I go to the game and our school is playing yours, which team should I cheer for?"

"I'll let you decided that, lady. Just sit behind me. That way, if you cheer for the opposite team, everyone will look at you funny." He laughs and hugs her, then suggests that they go for a walk.

The next day, during basketball practice, Coach Wynn calls all the teammates together to inform them of the starting five players. She tells the team that the schedule has been changed and the first game, which was a late agreement between her husband and herself, is against her husband's team, which is Shabazz High School girls' basketball team that is rated the number one girls' team in New Jersey.

The players laugh at the idea but show interest. They agree to it because the game would be the best girls' team against one of the worst boys' team in New Jersey. Mrs. Wynn informs Bob that he is no longer the team's captain. She chooses Ace as the new captain. Bob becomes furious and walks out of the gym, thinking that the only reason she chose Ace as the captain was because Ace is black. Four of Bob's friends leave with him as a sign of protest. The rest of the team look at one another, mumbling. The coach asks if there are any questions. When no one answers, she tells them that the game is being played tomorrow. With that in their minds, she dismisses the team.

After practice, Ace, Bayshawn, and Isaiah ride home with Joey again. Joey has convinced the coach that he is the right man for the manager's job by telling her that he will drive Ace and his friends home after practice. During the ride home, they have a change of heart about playing a girls' basketball team because of their ego. Isaiah and Bayshawn state that they're not going to play any girls regardless of how good they are. Ace tells them that if they don't play, then he won't play either. Ace has this great idea of who should be playing the girls' team by saying, "Let's tell the rest of the players to play Shabazz so that they can get their average score up because they might not be playing that much later on during the season. I'ma call the coach up later and tell her that."

Ace says to Joey, "How can I get a Benz like this to push in the hood?"

Joey tells him, "You got to hustle and get paid."

Isaiah asks Joey, "You sell drugs, Joey?"

"No, Isaiah. Selling drugs is for lowlife people.

"Lowlife? What do you mean by lowlife?" Bayshawn asks.

"You know. Those that don't have no dignity and don't care about who they're trying to destroy as long as they're getting paid. I mean, how low can you get if you don't care?"

Ace contemplates on what Joey said as he thinks about the offer Rock made to him. While in their neighborhood, Isaiah becomes excited over a young woman of color whom he usually sees waiting at the bus stop after practice while riding with Joey. He never mentioned her before or asked his friends if they noticed her.

Isaiah tells Joey with excitement, "Hey, Joey, slow down and stop in front of this shorty. Slow down, Joey, Slow down. I'ma holla at her."

"What shorty? What you talking about?"

"On your right at the bus stop. Slow down and stop the car."

Ace looks at her and says, "You just want to front with her so she can see you in a Benz."

Joey asks Isaiah, "What's up with her? Do you know her?"

Isaiah rolls down the window as the car approaches her and says to her, "Hello. I'm just speaking to you because every time I ride by here, it always looks as if you had a long, hard day. So, hopefully, a kind word might cheer you up."

The lady smiles a little and says, "Thanks, I did have a long day."

Isaiah tells her, "Well, your smile just helped brighten my day."

With that, she smiles again and thanks him.

Bayshawn tells Isaiah, "That might be somebody's woman."

"If it is, he's properly not treating her right and making her happy," Isaiah responds. "Because if he was, she would be smiling all day long even at work, thinking about him. Every time I see her, she looks as if she's upset."

Ace says, "Maybe she needs you to make her happy, Isaiah."

Joey tells them, "Maybe her man knows how to treat her, but she wants too much."

Isaiah responds by saying, "It might not be that she wants too much. It might be that she wants what she's supposed to have, and he's not providing for her. If I see her here again tomorrow, I'm getting on the bus with her and exchange numbers."

Ace tells Isaiah, "Go head and put your mack down."

Ace sees his prospective business partner Rock, the drug dealer. Ace thinks about all the "get rich quick" opportunities he missed out on while he was incarcerated. Now that he's out, he sees that the potential to get paid fast money is with Rock. Ace's thoughts are on driving himself to and from school in his own Benz with twenty-inch rims on it. This is the dream of a lifetime for some impoverished young inner-city adults who are not looking at the end results of selling drugs. The opulent lifestyle omits the thought of incarceration or death. They only see themselves as having a status in the hood as getting paid. Ace's thoughts of getting fast money has come to fruition with Rock.

Ace asks Joey to stop the car so that he could holler at him to see what's up. As Joey lets him out, Isaiah and Bayshawn are wondering why Ace wants to talk to Rock, knowing Rock's reputation. Ace shakes hands with Rock to establish a relationship so that Ace can introduce Rock's drugs to the students at West Winsor High School. After the deal was made, Ace leaves and walks to Fran'Sheila's house.

After greeting her, he says, "What's good, lady?"

"I was just thinking about you, Ace."

Ace smiles while thinking about the deal he made with Rock. "Hey, in a minute, I'm gonna be getting paid, and I'ma let the money pile up.

"How? By being student council president?"

Ace hesitated to respond and said, "Well, yeah."

Fran'Sheila says to him, "I know that's right. Just don't let it get to your head."

"I know what I'm doing," he said, but he was not really sure if he should put her up on what he's really getting into.

On the morning of the game with the girls' team, Ace tells Bayshawn that he has a business run with Joey, so he won't be making the game. The business run is really with his boy Rock. Yesterday, Bayshawn refused to play against the girls. But this morning, he tells Ace that he will be playing against them to represent the team. They shake hands, and Ace leaves. During the school day, the coach looks for the team and finds only five players. Obviously, Ace is not there. Bob caught feelings and is still upset. He told some of his friends (the ones that walked out of practice with him) not to show up as a form of protest because Coach Wynn took his captain's position from him.

The game starts after school that day with only five players. The coach is upset. The referees are a man and a woman. The boys had never played a game that wasn't physical before, so as they play with the girls, they have to play timid. They are afraid to touch the girls in order not to foul out. Four boys are playing with four fouls from playing too physical with the girls. Being in the position that they are in with four fouls, they try not to play too close to the girls to avoid fouling out. If one player would foul out, the game would have been forfeited. By playing that way, the girls outscore them and win the game by seven points.

While at home, Coach Wynn is feeling depressed, frustrated, mad, and upset. She takes her frustration out on her husband, who is in a state of euphoria because his team has beaten a boys' team. He realizes the hurt his wife is feeling, so he tries to console her.

"Hey, honey, you'll be feeling the same way I'm feeling when you win your first game too. Please don't be mad at me forever."

She walks away with a disgusted look on her face and says, "I'm mad at myself, so leave me alone!"

"Hey, I'll leave you alone in a few. But I want you to know that I will help you win the rest of your games because I know your mistakes, and I took advantage of your mistakes the same way other coaches will when you play your next game. I have the experience if you let me help you."

She tells him, "How can I get my team to win games when I can't even get them to come to a game? What kind of coach does that make me? The teammates all hate each other. The other day, when I got a new team captain, the old captain became indignant and walked out of practice. Some of the players are boycotting the games because they want the old captain back. Then the media treats me as if I'm their worst enemy. I know they'll write a front page article, criticizing me as a coach. Everyone's laughing at me now. I'm not giving them any interviews. And I'm—"

He puts his finger gently to her lips to stop her from talking and tells her, "You're going to have to learn how to be like a sponge and absorb the criticism. Every coach is criticized. I get criticized too. That's expected by a coach."

She starts to cry and says, "They haven't even given me a chance."

"Well, they're not going to give you a chance. You have to give yourself a chance to prove to yourself that you can bring this team together. Tomorrow, have a team meeting and ask the players, one at a time, why they lost. When everyone reaches an agreement on the loss, work on that. Tell them that every team is going to look at them as if they're soft, just like they did last year. So now your team is going to have a lot to prove. From the way you talked about the team, it sounds as if you have a good team. I have faith in you, but you're going to have to have faith in yourself."

"I have faith in myself. It's the team that needs to have faith in themselves. I'll talk to them so that they won't have any doubts about themselves to play as a team," she says. "I want a rematch with all of my team there this time. Then we'll really see who's the best."

He looks at her as if she was crazy. "Now, dear, you lost the game, lost the bet we had, and now you're losing your mind because we already know who has the best team." He laughs.

The next morning, Ace and Isaiah are on their way to West Winsor, riding on the bright yellow bus. Nobody knows who won the game because no one on the bus was at the game. Bayshawn and Squib played in the game, but they rode to school in a friend's car. Ace and Isaiah are on the bus assuming their team won and are wondering by how much.

Bob is walking to school wearing his team jacket. Just about every car and bus that drives by him has students in it pointing and laughing at him. Bob waves back and smiles, not knowing that they're laughing at him because his team lost to a girls' team. He comes to a corner to cross the street as the traffic light turns red. While standing at the corner, he glances at a newspaper that's in a newspaper vending machine. On the cover of the paper, the headline is printed in big black letters: west winsor high boys lose to a girls' basketball team.

The news media is male dominated and biased against West Windsor High due to the newly appointed female principal, who refuses to allow the media inside her school. They're vindictive against Mrs. Esteves and her African American coach. So regardless of what positive things happen, negative commentary statements will dominate the subject.

After Bob reads the headline, the light turns green as Bob walks across the street and reaches the other side before realizing what he has just read. He stops walking and says out loud in disbelief, "They lost?" He turns around and goes back across the street, repeating, "They lost?" The light turns red and catches him in the middle of the street. Finally, he reaches the paper machine, puts in some money, gets the paper, and reads it. As he's reading the paper, students are riding by in buses and cars pointing and mocking him. Bob realizes why they're mocking him, so he takes off his basketball team jacket and walks back across the street. When Bayshawn, Ace, and Isaiah reach the school with their team jackets on, they are ridiculed too.

All the team members receive a text from Joey to meet on the football field behind the school. When all assemble, the players that played were angered by the fact that they were the only players at the game. So they criticize those that weren't there, and those that weren't there are criticizing the players that played and gave them a bad reputation for losing. Both sides get into a pushing-and-shoving match. The police arrive, but before they do, one of the players leave the group, walks in the direction of the police car, and tells the police what's happening with the players on the bleachers. The police get out of their car and approach the team while they are still arguing. One of the cops is Chief Johnson, who played on this same ball team thirty years ago. This is the same chief who convinced the rioters not to riot at the beginning of the school year. In the background are the school security guards walking toward the bleachers too. The team members start to calm one another down and become silent as the chief approaches.

Chief Johnson says to them, "I would suspect hooky playing, but you're still on school property. Maybe I should suspect that everyone's cutting class, but I see that you're wearing your team jackets. Then I say to myself, a team meeting, and yes, I'm right. How about that? I'm sure there's a lot to discuss after that hard game y'all played yesterday. Y'all almost beat them girls. Wow, almost beat them. But why do you guys have to beat up on each other just because some girls beat you in a game of basketball? Y'all should be very proud of each other because y'all almost won. Let me figure something out." The Chief removed his hat. "West Winsor didn't beat any boys' teams last year, so y'all played against a girls' team this year thinking that you might get a win. Then y'all lost to a girls' team, so that didn't work. Maybe y'all should play against an elementary school. Yeah, play against some eighth graders. That might work." The police begins to laugh. "If the girls beat you and you're acting this way, what's going to happen when you lose against the elementary team?" The police laughs again. Some members of the team begin to leave until the chief tells them to sit down.

"Now everybody's blaming everybody else for the loss. But the school and the community is blaming the whole team for the loss. So as a team, you're going to have to put the blame on yourselves for losing. When you win, you win as a team because in a game, if you're there, playing or not, everyone is a part of that team. At the end of the season, this loss should be your only loss. Never forget the pain and never forget the loss. This is the last year for you seniors, so make a difference this year."

The team members looked at one another with disappointed faces, still not saying a word.

The police talks with the security guards before leaving. The security guards inform the players that when the next class period starts, they better be in class. Then the guards leave. After the guards and police leave from the bleachers, the team sits there without saying a word. Then Bob looks at Ace and says, "Hey, captain, this is your team, and it looks like it's going down already. When I was captain—"

Bob's friend stops him from finishing by saying, "Let's not start that again. Ace is the captain now, so let's see what he wants us to do."

Another teammate snaps back, "How is he going to want us to come to a game when he doesn't even show up to play."

Ace stands up, knowing that he has to take the lead in responsibility and says, "All right, my bad. We lost it.

Those that played the game lost, and those that didn't play lost out on the opportunity to play. I lost because I failed as a team leader and didn't give the team my support. I took the opposing team for granted, thinking that it was an easy win for us. But now I see that no team is an easy win for us. It's how we play the other team that's going to determine if we win. So as a team, we all failed. Look at us now. When we first got these jackets, we felt important to play for this school, to represent this school. Now we let some girls beat us. But it's not the jackets that's going to win the games for us. It's how we play the game. We should take this loss and make it our only loss. And it should be our only loss. Now we got the whole state looking at us, laughing. When this season is over, we should be laughing back at them with back-to-back wins. I know that the coach is hurting. Especially about what they wrote in the newspapers about her. About how a woman can't coach a boys' ball team. We owe it to her and to ourselves to make a difference this school year. We all got laughed at this morning. They didn't pick and choose who to laugh at. They just laughed at any player that was wearing a team jacket. So, fellows, let's take the ridicule for today, and let the people have their fun. But let's make the rest of the games ours. Put your jackets back on and walk through the halls with your heads up. This will be the only loss we'll suffer from any school. Do y'all feel me on this?"

Isaiah answers, "Yeah, I'm feeling you."

One at a time, the other members of the team, including Bob, stand up and put their jackets back on, saying, "Yeah, we're feeling you on that, Ace."

They huddle together in a circle, stick one hand out and grab someone else's hand while in that circle, count to three, and holler, "West Winsor High!" The school bell rings, and they walk off the field and into the school with their jackets on the rest of the day. This was the method of operation that the team used for the rest of the season.

Inside the school, Ace goes to the gym to talk with the coach in her office. Coach Wynn looks at him with a stern look on her face, without saying a word as Ace walks in. Ace knows that she's upset, so he asks her to let him talk. He asks for her permission to speak without her criticism because the team faced criticism all morning from the media and students. She agrees and allows him to speak.

"I know that there's a lot on your mind, but I don't need to be hollered at to understand how you feel. I appreciate the opportunity you gave me to be the team's captain because I've never been a leader before. But now I know what a leader's job consists of. As captain, I failed to lead. So as captain, I realize that I have to be responsible in my position. I've already talked to the team, and we have all admitted our mistakes. We made a promise not to ever put you in this situation again. I'm asking you to give me another chance to prove to myself and to the team and, above all, another chance for us to prove to you that we're a winning team. By doing this, we can show the critics that you can coach a team that has the potential to contend with any team in the state."

He pauses for a second and says, "Please give us another chance?"

Coach Wynn thinks about it for a few and tells him, "Well, there's a lot that I would like to say, but since you recognized your mistake, I'll postpone my words until you lose again. I did pick you as captain because I thought you were a leader. I'll find out by the end of the next game if you are. So I'll give you another chance, but don't disappoint me again."

Coach Wynn says this as a warning to Ace. After receiving criticism all day while wearing their team jackets, the team holds practice that afternoon after school. The coach sits on the bench, refusing to talk to the players as the team shoots baskets on the court. When the players approach her individually, she tells them that she doesn't want to talk. They walk away confused and begin to talk to one another, wondering why she is acting that way. Ace tells them that she will talk when she's ready. Until then, don't bother her.

Ace says, "It's not anything that I said to her. It's what we did that got her this way."

While the team continues to warm up, the coach blows her whistle. The players walk over to her on the bench. Everyone sits on the bench looking at her while she paces back and forth in front of them without saying a word. Her eyes stare at the floor as she paces. She looks up at the lights on the ceiling, and without looking at the team, she says, "Let's talk about the game we played yesterday."

"Ace!" she shouts as if he better know the answer to her question. "How did we lose the game?"

Ace tells her, "By a lack of leadership."

"Bob!" she hollers. "How did we lose the game?"

Bob's reply is, "By a lack of participation."

"Isaiah, how did we lose the game?"

Isaiah states, "By a lack of determination."

"Bayshawn, your opinion?" she asks.

His reply is, "By a lack of teamwork."

She asks the rest of the players the same question, and everyone gives her an answer. Coach Wynn tells them that their schedule will get harder with each game because they're playing from the weakest team to the best. Then she asks them, one at a time, starting from the last player she asked to the first, "Chris, what's going to prevent us from winning any games?"

She asks this question so that the players will have confidence in themselves. Chris's reply is, "Well, if we play hard and if—"

She stops him from finishing and tells him to run up and down the bleachers. She asks another player what is going to prevent them from winning any games. His answer is, "If the other team is better than us—"

She interrupts his answer and tells him to run up and down the bleachers too. She walks back and forth in front of them, staring at the floor again. The team is perplexed, and the players just look at one another. Coach Wynn then hollers at Ace, without looking at him, in the same you-better-have-the-right-answer tone, "What's going to prevent us from winning any more games?"

Everyone looks at Ace. Ace looks at the two players running up and down the bleachers. Then he stares at the coach, hoping that he gives her the right answer, and says, "Nothing."

Everyone waits for her reaction. She asks Bob the same question, so Bob repeats to her the same answer Ace gave, "Nothing is going to prevent us from winning any more games." The rest of the players sitting on the bleachers concur with that statement and gives her the same answer. This reply will echo in their minds throughout the season, starting from that day.

Three of the team players, Ace, Bayshawn, and Bob, go to the opposing school team to put themselves on display, wearing their West Winsor High School jackets. The other school laughs at them and reminds them that they were beaten by a girls' team. West Winsor beat that school by the score of 126 to 37. A week later, they repeat their tactic and beat the opposing team 102 to 25. With each school, they repeat the same tactic until their record is nineteen wins and one loss.

After each game, the local newspaper only lists the name of the school they play and the score. There are no write-ups or commentaries. Neither the team nor the coach receives any special write-ups. The team is upset. They attempt to talk to the newspaper's sports editor about it but were told by the editor, "No comment."

The coach holds a team meeting after practice and asks the team for a solution for them to gain state recognition. Ace tells the coach that they don't need any newspaper for recognition because their recognition is on the streets. When the coach and the rest of the team ask him what he means by that statement, he tells them that they will have to wait and see.

While riding home in Joey's car, Bayshawn asks Ace the same question the coach asked. Ace gives him the same answer while sitting at a traffic light on Greenwood Avenue looking at a billboard at a gas station that has a phone number on it with the words Advertise Here. The next morning, Ace and Joey ask the principal, Mrs. Esteves, for the approval to advertise on that billboard. She gives them her approval and signs her name on the check they have drawn out of the student council's funds. Even though Joey is the treasurer and Ace is the student president, no funds can be released from the account without the principal's approval.

They went to the agency to rent the space, and by the end of the day, the billboard on the corner a few blocks from Central High School has written on it in bold black letters, west winsor high basketball team, 19 and 1—#1 team in the state of nj.

The next day, that billboard causes a traffic jam on that corner and a sense of euphoria at West Winsor High school. The coach, principal, and team are outside reading the sign with all smiles. The school has this billboard under contract so that a new number will be added to it as they win. Ace, Bayshawn, and Bob go to another school to advertise their team, wearing their school jackets prior to playing that school that evening and beating them by thirty-three points. They repeat this until their team's record is twenty-three and one with the billboard showing it.

Central High's basketball team is returning from a game when they drive toward this same billboard. Central is the number-one-rated team in New Jersey. The coach sees it as they pass by it and becomes indignant at what he sees written on the billboard. He orders the bus driver to stop in the middle of traffic and rushes from the bus with his team following in disbelief. All of them are standing outside the bus, staring at the sign, complaining about who is the number one team in the state of New Jersey.

The team's center, Abdul, throws a brick at it, but a thin screen is protecting it against vandalism. The local newspaper doesn't even have West Winsor High School rated in the state or local area, saying that they haven't really played against any good or top-rated schools. West Winsor has played and beaten all the top-ten teams in the state except Camden and Central High School, but the media refuse to give them credit or recognition. West Winsor High also won their school's division too. Their next two games will be for the state championship.

CHAPTER 5

Ace is at home when Fran'Sheila visits him to discuss their relationship. Their relationship has cooled off since he became a businessman. With a disgusted look on her face, she says to him, "Ace, we haven't been seeing each other. What's occupying your time that stops you from seeing me? I've called you and left messages, and you didn't return my calls. All I wanted was to hear your voice, that's all."

He responded, "Yeah, I've been busy."

"Are we going to spend some time this evening, Ace?"

"Naw, we'll spend some time tomorrow, I promise."

With those words, she leaves the house shaking her head in disbelief, knowing that he's lying. Ace answers his cell phone and tells the caller that he is on his way out and that he has the money with him. The doorbell rings and Bayshawn walks in. After greeting each other, Bayshawn walks over to the window and looks out of it.

"What's poppin', Bayshawn?"

Bayshawn tells him, "You're what's poppin'. Everybody's talking about you. Your girl has been asking about you too. I mean you are the man, and you got it going on, but now you're starting to act stupid. And the bad part about it is you're starting to bring me down with you. You know we're tight because we grew up together. But you're letting some clown bring you down to ignorance."

"Hold it. What's up? What do you mean by somebody bringing me down to ignorance?"

"Ace, look at you. You don't have time for your family or your girl."

"You crazy. I just seen her. She just left from here. I'm not going to see her every day. I'm not in love, Bayshawn."

"Yes, you are. You're in love with Rock. You're selling crack for him. And you're probably using it too. I don't need any crackhead walking with me."

"What! I ain't no crackhead."

Bayshawn shouts back at him. "You're a fool, Ace. He's not doing nothing but using you. Then when he gets finished using you, he'll call the police on you and tell them that you're the major drug dealer so that he won't go to jail. Ace, Rock will give you money, but when the heat comes on him, he'll snitch on you. Then he'll laugh at you, and you don't even see that."

Ace looks at Bayshawn as if to say, "Are you finished?" but Bayshawn continues, "You used to be sharp yo, but now you're being played. This is going to put you back in jail."

Ace becomes fed up with the so-called big-brother talk and tells Bayshawn, "Selling dope ain't my life. I'm just selling it in school. And I don't need you to be telling me what I should be doing neither."

"Ace, somebody needs to be telling you what you should be doing because you acting stupid. Being with Rock is going to get you killed out here. And if you get shot, remember what I just said."

Ace snatches his keys off the table and asks Bayshawn, "Are you finished? 'Cause I got a business deal to go to."

Bayshawn gives up on his relationship with Ace to avoid any association with a drug dealer. "Yeah I'm finished. All we have in common is basketball, and you won't even last in that 'cause you're a crackhead."

Bayshawn looks at him for a short while without saying a word, and then he leaves.

The next day, Central High's coach, John, is still furious about West Winsor High's advertisement of their school being "number one" in the state. John is receiving funds from colleges throughout the country to encourage his top senior players to attend their colleges. Universities are interested in his players, but now he's afraid that the attention is going toward West Winsor's team because of their team record. Coach John has made a deal with St. John's University and some organized crime families in his area to encourage his top-three players to enroll into selected schools. John would receive a $25,000 bonus. But now he's intimidated by West Winsor High because they're receiving a lot of attention from basketball scouts from around the country.

Coach John discusses the advertisement with the mayor of Trenton, New Jersey, as they stand outside of city hall.

"That is a disgrace to the eyes of public. They have fabricated this malicious propaganda just to get a name for themselves."

The mayor's car pulls up, and he offers the coach a ride with him. They ride around the city while John is still voicing his frustration.

"Can't we sue for false advertising or defaming our name or something? They know that we are the best team in the state. We haven't even lost a game. We're still undefeated since last year. They really haven't even played us yet. Besides, they got beaten by a girls' basketball team. And yet they claim to be the best in the state. My team was so good. I gave them a couple of my players, and we're still undefeated. They're not even rated as a team in the sports section. So you know that they don't even count as a team."

The mayor tells the driver to pull over and stop the car. They get out and walk over to a man that is about sixty-nine years old sitting in Faircrest Park. As Coach John continues to complain to the mayor, the mayor smiles at the man and talks to him. "Hey, Joe, I heard you were looking for me."

The man smiles and tells the mayor, "Yeah, I was looking for you. I need a job. What can you do for me?"

"Joe, I can make it happen for you."

Joe begins to smile as the mayor tells him, "Since you're always in this park, your job is to keep this park clean. Just pick up the trash and the broken glass in the mornings. That's your job, Joe, so that the kids won't be playing in the glass, cutting themselves up. I will only be paying you part-time. You can start today but come down to my office to fill out an application, all right?"

"That'll work, Mr. Mayor."

They shake hands, and the mayor leaves. While walking back to the car, the mayor tells John, "You know, that used to be a beautiful park. I used to play ball on that court back in the day. I ain't saying that I was one of the best ballplayers out here, but I did a little something with the ball. I lived right up the street from here, growing up in Wilbur Section."

John says, "Faircrest Park still is beautiful. The glass and trash is making it look bad, that's all." John asks the mayor, "So what do you think we should do about that school?"

"I don't know, John. Anybody could claim to be number one. But proving it is what counts, isn't it?"

"Well, they haven't even proved it yet."

"Did your team played them yet?"

"No. They're not considered a team. It would probably ruin our reputation."

"This is what I'll do for you, John. I'll call their mayor up and see what he has to say about this."

The mayor calls up the mayor of West Winsor Township, talks with him for a few minutes, and then tells him that he'll holler at him later.

"Well, John, their mayor said that you were afraid to play them out of fear that you might get spanked like the rest of the teams that played against them. That's why they consider themselves the number one team in New Jersey."

John is shocked and tries to talk, but the mayor stops him and says, "Hold it, John. That's not all. He said if you have any doubts about his team being number one, then put your money up and get with his team on the ball court. If not, shut up and bow down to the kings of the court."

"He said that?" John asked with disbelief that another team has the audacity to challenge him. "Even their mayor believes that too, huh? They've got just one more team to play. And if they win, they'll be playing us for the state title. Then we'll just have to prove to the world the same way we've been proving to them. And after we beat them, get permission from their mayor to allow my team to tear down that billboard."

After school at Central High, Fran'Sheila is waiting for Ace at his usual spot at the bus stop. The bus Ace is on is at the red traffic light and is in Fran'Sheila's sight. Rock, who has become tight friends with Ace, has always disrespected Fran'Sheila. He is supposed to meet Ace there also. Fran'Sheila knows that Rock is a drug dealer, and she despises him. Rock walks up to her with a smile on his face and asks her, "Can I spend some time with you?"

He knows that Ace hasn't been seeing her, so he says this sarcastically. She asks him, "What do you mean by that?"

"I mean, as fine as you are, somebody is going to notice you. Ace don't. If he did, he'll be spending more time with you."

"Don't talk to me like that," she tells him angrily.

Rock ignores her words as he walks closer to her and says, "You know I'm starting to feel you," as he gently touches her face. She smacks the left side of his face with her right hand with the sound of it echoing through the crowd, so loud that it catches everyone's attention.

Rock, who is now embarrassed because of his reputation as a gangsta, attempts to retaliate, but he sees Ace walking off the bus toward them. He looks at Ace and then says to her, "I'll remember that hit when Ace drops you."

He means that as long as Ace and she are together, she is safe. Rock also is thinking about the money Ace is making for him at his school. She tells him, "You get dropped before I do."

When Ace reaches them, he grabs her, kisses her cheek, and hugs her while smiling. Ace talks to Fran'Sheila for a few, then he tells her that he has to make a run with Rock and that he'll talk to her later. After kissing her cheek again, Ace gives her a long hug. While hugging, Fran'Sheila stares at Rock. Ace kisses her again, and then he leaves with him.

Ace rides with Rock and his boys to pick up twenty kilos of cocaine from a distributor. Rock dealt with them before but on a lower level, just to test the quality of the coke. Ace is the driver in a crew of four. He drives to the house where the exchange is to take place. Rock and his boys get out and walk inside the house. As Ace waits inside the car, a blue four-door sedan with dark-tinted windows pulls up with the words 12Gauge on the license plate. Ace thinks about a twelve-gauge shotgun as he looked at the plate. In the hood, it's also known as a 12 Gotti. The driver of that car gets out and stands on the side of the car. The Italian occupants get out and walk inside the house where Rock and his crew are waiting. Rock calls Ace on his cell and tells him to drive around to the back of the house.

While sitting behind the house, he relaxes while checking out the surrounding sights. The sound of rapid gunfire interrupts his relaxation and causes him to panic as he moves his head from side to side, not knowing where the shots are coming from. Then the back door of the house opens with Rock and his boys walking out of it with suitcases in their hands. Rock tells Ace to open the trunk of the car by pushing the trunk release button. Rock throws the suitcases in the trunk, shuts it, and gets in the car with his crew. Ace drives away nervously and begins to sweat. He wants to ask them what happened, but he assumes that they think he should already know, so he doesn't say a word, especially when he looks at the expressions on their faces. So he keeps driving.

While driving back in the hood, he passes by Fran'Sheila, who is standing on the sidewalk in the neighborhood. Fran'Sheila sees Ace and starts to wonder what he is really doing with Rock. Ace doesn't see her because he's still nervous and trying to reach his destination so that he can get out of the car. Fran'Sheila now knows why her time has been cut short with Ace. It's because of Rock.

Mrs. Wynn is home with her husband, telling him about all the attention she is receiving from colleges and universities throughout the country. Her husband, Jim, tells her, "Hey! It's the billboard that's causing all of the attention. You're taking away all of Central's popularity."

She kisses him on the lips and says, "Thanks. All of the colleges are interested in my seniors. They're asking me when are we going to play Central High School and what are my chances of winning. I told them that Central High is thinking about forfeiting to us so that they won't have to face the embarrassment of losing this season on the court."

They laughed at that.

"St. John's University's coach called me to say that Central High's coach is hating on me and my team. He said Coach John said that I have a Cinderella team. And it's all just a dream for me to win against his team. I told him that Central's team is a 'has been' team that intimidates other teams into losing. I also told him that I build my team from nothing and made them the best team in the state. And I'll put everything behind them against any school in the nation. That's when he told me that he likes a person with confidence and said he'll be talking to me in the near future. Then the mayor called me to say that all of the outsiders have doubts about my team winning the state finals. He congratulated me and said he has confidence in me. I believe in my team, and they believe in themselves that we're going to win the state championship. And after I get that championship title, I'll be putting in my application for that coaching position at Rutgers University for the girls' basketball team. Just think about it. I'm only two games away."

Fran'Sheila visits Ace the next day out of concern for their relationship. She tells him that there's a change in him that's unusual and alludes to him about his company with Rock and their sordid illegal business. She also reminds him about the promises he made to her, saying that last night was supposed to have been their night to spend time together, but again, his broken promise left her all alone. She tells him, "Your friends are your choice. You're showing me who you really want to be with. Maybe I'm asking for too much. But I'm only asking because I care. Now if I'm wrong, let me know."

Ace tells her, "As I grow up in this world, I'm going to meet a lot of new people, lady. You're one of those new people too. If I gave everybody all of my time, it still wouldn't be enough. And I need time for myself too. I do choose people to kick it with, and I might make the wrong choice one day with one of those people. But let me decide who I want as my friends, and if I'm not feeling them, then I won't be with them."

Fran'Sheila assumes that he was talking about her too. But Ace assures her that he wasn't by grabbing her and kissing her cheek. Then he asks her to go shopping with him.

During practice the next day, Bayshawn and Ace are still not cooperating with each other on the court because of the beef they had the previous day. They're playing ball but not passing the ball to each other. This attitude goes on between them at every practice. Coach Wynn decides to talk to them about their attitude toward each other, but they told her that there was nothing wrong between them.

On the night of the semifinals game, the number two team in New Jersey, Camden High School, was leading by one point. With twenty seconds remaining on the clock, Bayshawn steals the ball from Camden High's guard and then passes the ball to Ace, who is running toward the basket. Ace goes up for a layup and cuffs the ball on his forearm as he rocks it and dunks it. The crowd goes crazy, knowing that an upset is imminent. There are ten seconds left on the clock and no time-outs for Camden when they inbound the ball. Camden is unsuccessful in scoring when the time expires. Camden loses by one point when the game is over.

While both teams are congratulating each other and walking off the court, Bayshawn walks over to Ace and tells him, "Don't say I ain't never gave you nothing. You should take my advice about Rock, like you took my pass, yo." Ace looks at him with a smirk on his face and walks off the court.

The next day after the game, Central High's Coach John receives a call from St. John's University's head coach. He complains about the talent his scout reported to him about West Winsor High School players. "John, you told me that woman's team players were bums. You said that team was whack. My scouts are telling me that they have the best guards and forward in the state. And what's shocking, John, is I was told that those players were from your school."

John is now worrying that he will be losing his bonus if the university isn't interested in his players. Last year, he received $15,000 for encouraging and sending one player to their university. This year, the amount could double if the university takes his two seniors.

"Yes, they were from my school, but they were my rejects. That's why I got rid of them. I know what's best for my team. That's why we're undefeated. And we're going to remain that way to repeat the state title. Besides, that team that lost to them yesterday, we beat them by ten points during the regular season. They lost by one yesterday. West Winsor High doesn't have a win with me, and you can put your money on it."

"Well, John, that's what we're planning on doing. I'll take your word on it. I'll get back with you, okay?"

"All right. Thanks for calling."

After they hang up, the St. John's University coach calls his friends in the mob and gives them the okay to place a bet on Central High School for the state title. The odds are six to one, favoring Central. The mob from North Jersey makes it known that the money is guaranteed because the senator is putting that bet money in an offshore account. Joey's father takes up on the bet also. He receives a phone call and meets with the North Jersey mob bosses at a restaurant to discuss the offer.

After greeting one another, they sit down to make the bet. Joey's father tells them, "Gentlemen, I don't know what you heard about me, but I don't make small bets. I have a lot of confidence in my son and his team. I appreciate the offer to do business with you." Joey

Senior proposes a toast with all glasses raised, "May the best team win." After the toast, they sip the champagne, recognizing the bet.

That Saturday evening, Ace is standing near the corner of Locust and Monmouth Streets with Rock and his boys, laughing and talking about their domain in the hood. They're bragging about the money they made and how big they want to be. Rock tells Ace that they have so much coke that he wanted Ace to recruit students at his school to sell coke on the streets of West Winsor Township. Rock has become a drug distributor to the majority of major gang leaders in south and central New Jersey. Rock has named himself the chief executive officer (CEO) of his franchise. He's hiring more young kids in the neighborhood as drug runners to accommodate the new customers as the business increases. Ace is enthralled by the street life and the fast money he's making on the streets of Trenton, New Jersey.

Fran'Sheila sees Ace at a distance from across the street and starts to walk toward the group. Rock sees her coming and says to Ace, while frowning, "Here comes your so-called woman."

She wants to ask Ace why he didn't come by last night and why he didn't answer his phone when she called. Fran'Sheila is aware that Ace is selling drugs for Rock and his time has been devoted to Rock. She excuses herself to everyone as she greets them and asks Ace if she could speak to him alone. Rock tells her, "We're busy." Then he tells Ace to leave the trash alone because they're getting paid now and that he don't need no neighborhood girl riding him. Rock hasn't forgotten the slap he received from her, so the vendetta is still against her. She looks at Rock without saying a word and asks Ace again if they could talk alone. Ace tells her to leave and that he'll holler at her later. She is shocked that those words came out of his mouth. The lady turns around in disbelief and walks away. But determination makes her turn back around to try desperately to convince Ace to leave Rock. Bayshawn tried previously to get Ace out of Rock's company by telling Ace that being with Rock was going to get him killed. Fran'Sheila's love for Ace turns her back around in a last-minute effort to get Ace to leave from the corner. She tells Ace as she begins to cry, "Rock is going to bring you down. He doesn't care about nobody but himself." As she slowly walks across the street backward, facing Ace, Fran'Sheila says to Ace, "You let an idiot control you. Rock is already speaking for you, and now he's controlling your life. Now you've become a nobody because you're hanging with a nobody."

Rock becomes furious and tells Ace to go over to her and punch her in her mouth because she's talking too much and disrespecting him. Fran'Sheila is across the street now, and Ace is pursuing her to punch her for disrespecting Rock. Ace once protected her from other dudes that were assaulting and disrespecting her. Now his love for mad money from Rock made him obligated to protect Rock from all insults as well as assaults. Regardless from whom the insults came, friend or foe, Ace is Rock's protection.

At this time, a blue four-door sedan is slowly cruising toward that corner. Ace is between the parked cars across the street as the sedan drives past him. He balls up his fist in anger, feeling that she is interfering with him getting paid. Ace was three feet away from Fran'Sheila when he told her she talks too much and was just about to slap her when he heard the sounds of twelve-gauge shotgun blasts behind him, being sprayed on Rock and his boys. As he hears the blasts, he turns halfway, but he is still in the thrust of swinging his hand. Fran'Sheila bends down to avoid the slap as Ace falls on top of her, knocking her to the ground with his upper chest. He lays there with his head tucked between his arms and covering her head until the shooting stops.

When it stops, the blue sedan speeds away. Ace lifts up his head to see who was doing the shooting. When he saw the car that has the words "12 gauge" on the license plate, he realizes that this is the same sedan that was in front of the house where Rock made his drug transaction and shot the men inside. Ace gets up to see Rock and his boys lying on the ground. He starts to walk toward them as he walks between the parked cars. Ace stops between the cars, turns and looks at Fran'Sheila, turns toward Rock, and takes another step into the street toward them and stops. He turns again and look at Fran'Sheila, this time thinking about what she said and what Bayshawn told him about how being with Rock was going to get him killed. After thinking about those words, he realizes that by being with Fran'Sheila (although he had negative motives for her), she saved his life.

Ace kneels down and starts to cry, knowing that he owes his life to her because she was right. Fran'Sheila walks over, kneels down with him, and begins to cry also. Bayshawn runs down the street and stands over Rock and asks what happened. The bystanders point in the direction that the car went. Ace's younger brother Tony arrives on the scene and sees Ace kneeling with Fran'Sheila, so he gets down with them. Bayshawn comes over and stands over Ace, who is still crying. Bayshawn wants to tell Ace, "See, I told you about Rock," but he turns around and looks at Rock again, then he walks away, shaking his head.

That weekend, Fran'Sheila and Ace have a lot to discuss about their relationship and how much they need each other. They become very tight friends again but this time stronger in their thoughts about each other. She instills in his mind about the importance of his academic and vocational education. While selling drugs, he cut class and sometimes never did his homework. She stresses to him that street knowledge or street education will benefit him for life on the streets. And academic and vocational education will allow him to ingratiate himself into the workforce. But the street life is the only life Ace knows how to live by. Fran'Sheila informs Ace that she has a very low tolerance for those who disrespect her. Then she gives Ace one warning: not to disrespect her with any of her enemies again. All his brothers' way of life was either in jail or on the street. His challenge is to break that cycle of life with a little help from his lady, and he is willing to win that challenge.

On Monday, at Central High School, while waiting for the bus to take them to West Winsor High School, Ace walks up to Bayshawn and speaks to him. But he can't find the words to tell him that he was right about his so-called friend, Rock. The only words that stay on Ace's mind are "Being with Rock will get you killed." These words were what Bayshawn and Fran'Sheila repeated to him before the drive-by shooting. Bayshawn just watches as Ace tries to articulate his feelings. When he sees that Ace can't talk and only manages to bow his head toward the ground and shake it, he tells Ace, "Don't worry about that, yo. You're here with us, and that's what counts. They lived on the blocks, and they died on the blocks. We still got to take this state title from this school. Are you with me on that?" They shake hands and give each other a half hug. Ace looks at Central High and thinks about his school's ball team, then he walks on the bus.

After school, during practice, all the players are assisting each other to get their skills tight for the game against Central High on Friday. Some are showing others how to rebound against Central. And other players are showing how to play defense on Central's guards. Central is known for having the best defensive team in New Jersey. Coach Wynn thinks about making her team the fastest team in the state, taking that reputation away from Central High. While watching the players, she blows her whistle. Everyone assembles on the bench with excitement. She tells them while pacing back and forth, looking down at the floor, "I'm going to get everyone ready for Friday night's game."

Coach Wynn calls out her starting five players and tells them to put on the red shirts. Then she calls out another five players and tells them to put on blue shirts. When Ace, Bayshawn, Isaiah, Squib, and Bob feel comfortable with whom they are about to play, she called an extra player and tells him to put on a blue shirt too. The five starters are puzzled, looking at the six players that are about to play against them on the court. The coach tells the blue team to double-team the ball every time the starting five dribbles the ball.

The five against six didn't seem fair. While playing, Ace's team loses the ball from the pressure of the blue team. Coach Wynn blows her whistle and tells Ace, "That's what you'll be facing when you play Central. Let's try it again."

Isaiah looks at Ace and tells him, "Give me the ball. I'll be the point guard." This works for the starting five. They beat the trap and begin to score. When any of them gets tired, a substitute is called in to take their place. This is the coach's special offensive play. She then tells her starting five to set up for a center trap. All the players are spread at a distance down the middle of the court. Two players trap the ball while the other three players read the offense. They practice figuring out whom the ball will be thrown to before the opposing players throw it in order to steal the ball. This works too, but it's very tiring. They continue to practice this way for the rest of the week.

Finally, it's Friday morning, the day of the game. Around 10:45 a.m., Ace, Bayshawn, and Joey are sitting at a table in the cafeteria, discussing their chances of winning the state title. Ace and Bayshawn are convinced that they have no win against their former school. They know that all of Central's players can score an average of thirty points against them. Joey doesn't care who wins; he just want to bet on somebody. Joey tells them about the odds on the game, and he tells them as of today, Central is a ten-to-one favorite. Ace thinks about those odds and thinks about the drug money he no longer makes, since getting out of the drug business, and suggests to Joey, "So let's bet on Central High."

Bayshawn asks, "For what? We ain't Central."

Ace tells him, "So that if we lose, we can still come out as a winner, you feel me?"

Bayshawn thinks about it, and Joey doesn't mind because all Joey wants is to get paid. So Joey asks Ace, "How much are we going to bet?"

Ace asks Joey, "How much do we have in the student council account?"

"Fifty thousand dollars!" Joey shouts back.

Ace looks at him and says, "Okay, let's bet that."

"But, Ace, how are we going to withdraw it without the principal's signature? I'm not forging her name on the check."

"Listen, Joey, tell the principal that we would like to transfer the account to that bank that helps students with student loans and scholarships. You know, the one downtown. That way, all three of our signatures will be on the withdrawal slip check and close the account. Tell the bank to give you a certified check, then take the check down to the betting station and place the bet on Central, yo."

Joey is elated as if this is the greatest day of his life, betting with $50,000. Bayshawn tells them, "Yeah, that's good money. But I would rather bet against those odds and play a little harder."

Ace tries to convince Bayshawn by saying, "Do you see what we're up against, yo?"

"Yeah, I see it. I just don't want to give them bragging rights for the summer, talking about how they repeated winning the title again."

Joey's mind is made up. "I'll go tell the principal now about the transfer."

He stands up and begins to leave when Ace stops him and says, "This subject is just between the three of us. Because it's just the three of us who will be splitting the winnings, you feel me?"

Joey goes to get the principal's signature. After she signs the withdrawal slip, he finds Ace, and both of them sign it. With the three signatures on the slip, Joey leaves to place the bet. Prior to leaving the school, Joey goes to the library to return a book. The real purpose of him going to the library is to place more bets on the game with his own money. He texts all his contacts in school and makes it known that he's taking all bets in the library. As he enters the library, one of his contacts comes in after him to place a bet with him. This student is six feet five inches tall and weighs 275 pounds. When he comes inside the library, he is stopped by the librarian who is a sixty-four-year-old woman weighing about 105 pounds. She asks him, "Young man, why aren't you in class at this time?"

His response is, "I was on my way home, but I decided to come to the library to get a book about basketball so that I could understand the game a little bit better tonight."

He tells her this while looking over her head, trying to find Joey.

"No one is allowed in the library unless they have a pass or they're returning a book."

"Oh, I didn't know that. I apologize, and I promise that the next time I come in here, I will have a book in my hand, if you allow me to borrow one this time, please."

She allows him to get a book with a warning not to come again without a pass or a returned book. Then she directs him to the sports section. He borrows a paperback book entitled *How the Game of Basketball Is Played*. Before he leaves the library, he places his bet with Joey. As he walks toward the door, the librarian stops the student and tells him to take good care of the book and not to rip it.

"It will be safe with me at all times. I'll even bring it to the game tonight," he says while walking out the door.

CHAPTER 6

At about 12:00 p.m., Ace, Bayshawn, Bob, and Isaiah arrive at Central High to do their usual advertising by wearing their team jackets. The school jackets are bright, and the name West Winsor High School is on the back of the jackets. While inside the school, they go to the principal's office with their jackets off. The principal recognizes Bayshawn and Isaiah, then gives them all passes to visit their former basketball coach. Their intentions are not to visit the coach but to let the students know that West Winsor High is in the place, and they aren't afraid of them, on or off the court.

After receiving the passes, they walk through the halls with their jackets on, receiving mad attention. Bayshawn escorts them to the cafeteria where Central's team players' hangout is. All the students are excited about tonight's game. The music is playing; students are dancing and laughing as they talk about taking the state title again. Just about all of Central's team is in the cafeteria. Class wasn't essential to Central players this day because all the festivities are in the cafeteria.

As Ace and his team walk in the cafeteria from one end to the other, the noise begins to fade. All eyes are on the four West Winsor players. The music stops as they get closer to the table where Central players are sitting. They reach the table reserved for the players. The Central players demand to have this section of tables by threatening the other students sitting there. Abdul, a six-foot-eight senior who plays center for Central, is in the middle of a conversation about how they're going to beat West Winsor High tonight until he sees Ace and his boys walking toward them. He stops talking and asks his team, "What they doing here?"

The rest of Central's students are surprised to see West Winsor players at their school too. Along with the rest of the players, Abdul stands up, displaying his 254-pound, six-foot-eight-inch body. Abdul tells them as they approach the table, "We don't allow advertising in our school, and you know that, Bayshawn."

Bayshawn tells him, "We're not advertising. We just came to holla at y'all before the game, and we come in peace."

"Then what's with the jackets?"

Bob responded to him by saying, "It's cold outside. We got to wear something."

Abdul tells Bob, "Ain't nobody asked you nothing. You can't speak in my school."

Ace interjects, "Hold it, gentlemen. We don't want no trouble. We apologize if we offended anyone. We come to holla at your coach and congratulate him for making the finals, yo."

"Y'all can't walk through here with your jackets on. Bayshawn, how are you going to do what we do and take it to another school? That's our work, yo."

Bob asks Abdul, "So what you saying? Is this illegal or something? We from West Winsor High, and we walk the way we feel like walking."

The students stand up from the tables and start to circle around the players as Abdul shouts back at Bob,

"I told you not to speak. Now say something else. I'ma touch your cheek when I drop this right hand on you."

Bob displays no fear when he states, "You got a cheek too, so what's up?"

Abdul walks toward Bob as they begin to argue. Then a shouting match begins between the two teams. Security is called to escort Ace and his team out among a hostile crowd of students shouting, "We're number one!"

At 1:30 p.m., Joey drives up in front of the numbers shop to place the bet on Central High. His attention is distracted by a large crowd of people from across the street. There are police vehicles, fire trucks, and ambulances at the scene. He notices a man sitting on the edge of the roof with a cop near his side talking. Some people in the crowd are begging him not to jump, and some are telling him to jump. Joey looks at his watch and takes a deep breath. He then hollers to a friend a short distance away, "If he was going to jump, he would have done it by now. He just wants some attention."

"Naw, Joey. The man said when the camera crews come, he's jumping. And the media just showed up," Joey's friend shouts back.

Joey has doubts about the man jumping, so he pulls out a fifty-dollar bill and said, "Fifty dollars he won't jump."

"Bet, Joey. I'll take your money."

The crowd is saying in unison, "Jump, jump, jump." Then another man shouts to Joey, "I'll bet you fifty." These men know that Joey is the neighborhood bookie, and the store Joey's parked in front of is the store where all the numbers are placed. Joey looks around as he holds his fifty over his head and says to the crowd, "Fifty dollars, anyone?"

After taking five bets, he asks for more bets until the police, who are observing him engaging in his illegal activities, apprehend him. Joey tries to run but fails and is charged with illegal gambling, interfering with the duties of an officer, encouraging bodily harm, and disorderly conduct. The bet on the school's game must be made an hour before starting time, and it's approaching 2:00 p.m. Starting time for the game is at 7:00 p.m. Since he is seventeen years old, Joey must be released to a parent or guardian. The dilemma for him now is that he doesn't want to tell his mom that he's in jail because she told him that she trusted him. So he tries to get in touch with his father. But his father is not trying to hear about him going to jail for something stupid. So Joey calls the family attorney and leaves a message for him about his situation and asks that he get him out of jail and not to get his father involved with this.

About 4:30 p.m., Mrs. Wynn is at home accepting congratulations from friends who telephoned her to wish her well with the game. Her husband congratulates her after she hangs up the phone. He tells her, "Dear, this is the part of the season when butterflies get into your stomach, making you a nervous wreck. This is when all of the training and instructions you gave all season depend on this one night. Tonight, you will know if you are as good a coach as you said that you could be. But even if you don't win, you know that within your heart, you went farther than your critics wanted you to go, and I'm proud of you."

She says, "Thanks. But if the team would only believe in themselves, they could win the championship."

"Well, dear, it's up to you to make them believe in themselves."

She nods her head and picks up a photo of the team and stares at it.

At about 5:00 p.m., Ace and Bayshawn are sitting on the porch, waiting for Joey to return from betting and to pick them up to take them to school to get ready for the game. Bayshawn becomes impatient as he looks around and asks Ace, "Where is this dude, yo? How long does it take to make a bet? Call him again. You should have went with him. He probably cashed the check and moved back to Italy. I never did trust him. We're gonna lose the game and the money. I ain't never lost $50,000 before."

Ace looks at Bayshawn as if he is crazy and tells him, "You ain't never had $50,000 before."

"If this idiot shows up, I'll have it by tonight." They laugh.

"So, Ace, how are we gonna do this? I mean, are we gonna just let them blow us out? I can't go out like that."

"We ain't going out like that, yo. We'll just be playing ball. In fact, we'll be playing hard, aggressive ball. But if we're winning in the fourth quarter, we'll just have to drop back and let them score some, that's all."

"That's too far-fetched 'cause they're going to get theirs regardless," Bayshawn tells him.

Ace stands up and sees Fran'Sheila walking across the street. "There's my angel, let me see if she can get her mom to ride us to school."

Bayshawn sees her and says, "Let's worry about the game later and see if we can find this dude with our money first."

At 5:30 p.m., Joey's father comes to the police station to bail him out. Joey is inside the jail cell trying to place bets on the game with the prisoners. The other prisoners don't have any sure way of paying up, so it's not possible for him to make any bets. Joey feels relieved when the officer calls him and tells him that his father is here. He leaves the cell, then signs papers to receive his property and goes out to meet his father. When he speaks to his father, his father does not respond but has a stern look on his face. While outside of the police station, Joey's father slaps him on the right side of his face and tells him that he talks too much. He criticizes Joey by saying, "You talk too much, and you're too loud. You can't let everybody know that you're placing bets. I never taught you that, did I? I always told you to keep a low profile and to be smooth with yourself. But you don't listen, do you?"

They get into the car and drive off, continuing with the conversation. "I never had to come to your school because you didn't behave, but here I am going to jail to get you out because you're running up and down the street making bets on some nut sitting on the roof."

Joey temporarily forgets why he was arrested until his father mentions the nut on the roof. "When you make a bet, you don't have to let everyone know about it," his father stated.

"Did that man on the roof jump?" Joey asks with excitement.

"Shut up when I'm talking. That's your problem now. You must have gotten that from your mother. Where's your car? Is it at school?"

"No, it's at the store. I was going to place a bet on the game, but I went across the street to see what was happening. Then I got picked up."

His father shakes his head in disgust and says, "Business first, Joey. Business."

He tells the driver to take them to the store. Joey Senior takes a deep breath and wags his head again, still disgusted by his son. He tells Joey, "You know, I've bet a lot of money on your school. I hope they pay off for me. You told me that your school is the best ball team in the state. So I put big money on y'all. I would hate to be disappointed."

They reach the store and go inside. Joey walks up to the man behind the counter without his father. He wants to place the bet and leave without his father knowing whom he placed the bet on. The man greets him and says, "How can I help you, Joey?"

"Well," Joey tells him, "West Winsor High is making history tonight, and I want to be a part of it. But I have devised a plan to make some money."

While Joey was talking to the man, his father walks in the store and toward them unknowingly. The man says to Joey, "So what are you implying? You only got about two minutes to place a bet, then the books are closed. How much are you betting?"

Joey pulls out the cashier's check and says, "Fifty thousand dollars," as he displays the check to the bookie. When the man asks whom he is betting on, Joey's father walks up and stands behind him, being indignant about the question, and tells him with anger, "West Winsor High School. That's who my boy represents. He's the team's manager. You're wasting our time. I'm a busy man.

We don't need to talk. Just put the bet in before it's too late."

Joey is shocked and tries to speak but can't. He starts sweating and his knees begin to shake. He hands over the check slowly as if he is trying to find an excuse not to bet on a team that is facing their demise. Prior to this, Joey talks his father into betting on his school, so he didn't want to disappoint him since his father put up mega bucks on his team. This dilemma is devastating to him because he doesn't want to upset his father any more than he already is. But he has to choose between his friends and the money or his father. Joey gives in and chooses to stick with his father, thinking that he can always get new friends. The man behind the counter takes the check, writes it down, slams the book shut, and says, "The bets are in. The bets are sealed. Here's your receipt and have a good day, gentlemen."

Joey's father says, "Thanks, we'll be collecting our money tomorrow." He grabs his son by the shoulder and turns him around. When he sees the look on Joey's face, he asks him what is wrong. Joey tells him that he never made a bet that large before and maybe he should just get it back.

"What? Are you crazy or something? Fifty thousand, thirty thousand, what difference does it make when you're betting on a winning team?" he says, smiling. "Forget about it. You'll be all right, son, when you collect." They walk out of the store when his father tells him again, "You'll be all right. Just stay out of trouble."

Joey walks past his car and continues to walk down the street, stomping and cursing at himself while walking into an alley. While in the alley, he picks up a garbage can and throws it, saying how stupid he is and what he should've done. He repeatedly asks himself why he let his father talk him into betting on West Winsor. He repeats this over and over until he finally sits on the ground in that alley, crying.

In the locker room, prior to the start of the game, Coach Wynn gives her team a pep talk about the game. After the talk, the team enters the floor to a mixture of cheers and boos. As the team warms up, Joey's father walks in with Bob's father, Patrick, who is the mayor of West Winsor Township. They find seats in the stand that are not too high. Directly across from them on the other side of the court are the mobsters from New York. Bob's father, Patrick, is in the bleachers, telling everybody that his son is the team's star player and that's why the team is where they are today. Central High enters on the ball court, and the crowd erupts with excitement. The pandemonium drowns out every conversation in the stadium. Central perform their prodigious layup drill that includes backward, forward, and sideway dunks, bringing the crowd off their seats.

Ace calls his team together and walks them up to the half-court line to observe Central's team as they practice their layups. Central becomes more arrogant, knowing that they're being watched by West Winsor. Ace, Bayshawn, and Isaiah point to the players on Central and tell their teammates how to play each one of them. After their brief discussion, West Winsor High turns around and continues with their layup drill. Coach Wynn shakes hands with all well-wishers and waves to the spectators. The horn blows, and both teams huddle up. West Winsor High is introduced first as the starting five is announced.

Coach Wynn has decided to try something new before the game starts. She tells Bob that he is not starting this game. He is surprised but goes with it because he wants to study the way Abdul plays on the court.

After the starting five is introduced, the mayor of West Windsor notices that his son isn't starting. He becomes furious and runs down to complain to the coach about this injustice. While Central is being introduced, the mayor approaches Coach Wynn and talks to her alone.

"Excuse me, Mrs. Wynn. But may I assume that you don't want that coaching job I promised you at Rutgers University?"

She tells him, "The deal has been made, and I haven't changed my mind yet, so I'm looking forward to my new job."

"Oh no, Mrs. Wynn. See, you just don't understand. The deal is that as long as you keep my son in the starting lineup during the regular season, you can look forward to a coaching job that's going to be vacant at Rutgers. And you blew that, lady."

She looks at him and shakes her head and says, "Did I say that your son would start in all of the regular season games, sir?"

"Yes, you did. And I don't see him starting. You blew it."

Coach Wynn tells him, "Mr. Mayor, this is not the regular season. This is the playoff."

She turns and walks back to her team, leaving Bob's father standing there, looking confused. When the mayor's friends ask him why his son isn't starting, his reply is that Bob's leg is hurting and the coach is saving him for the latter part of the game. The mayor is surprised at the size of Central's players. Joey's father asks if they are really students and begins to point at the players, asking how tall they are. The mob from New York sends over a pack of tissues and smiles when the messenger gives it to Joey's father as a gesture that he will be needing them after the game because of losing the bet. When the messenger points to where the tissues came from, Joey Senior throws the tissues down and grins over at the sender.

Ace asks his players if they know where Joey is because the game is about to begin. Bayshawn tells him, "Yeah, he's probably on a plane by now, and I hope it blows up." The rest of the players are wondering what he meant by that statement but didn't bother to ask.

Bob tells them, "We don't need him here. We got all ballplayers, and that's what counts. He's probably placing a bet somewhere." Bayshawn and Ace look at each other, thinking if Joey told him about their betting deal.

"Amir," Bob yelled. "Work on Abdul until I get in. Dee him up. He ain't got no game. Don't let him intimidate you."

The buzzer sounds again, and everybody stands up to give West Winsor and Central High an ovation. When the game starts, Central wins the tip-off and scores by a reverse slam dunk. This is the beginning of a fast-paced, run-and-thriller ball game between two teams who choose to be enemies for the duration of the game.

Abdul is still vexed about how West Winsor players disrespected his school by walking in the cafeteria, advertising WWHS on the backs of their jackets. Abdul trash-talks to Bayshawn and Ace on every play, verbalizing his anger. The head referee is paid off by the New York mob, so more violations are called on West Winsor's team than on Central's. When Bob enters the court, a pushing and shoving match commences between him and Abdul. Abdul tells him, "Coming to our school and trying to front with us didn't work. Y'all ain't really played nobody until today. We never got beaten by no girls' team, and we ain't going to let y'all girls beat us neither."

Abdul is in the inner lane under the basket when he reaches for the ball, and his teammate passes it to him. He takes two dribbles and backs Bob up a little before he swings his elbow, hitting Bob in the chest, knocking him to the floor. Then Abdul turns toward the basket and slam dunks the ball with two hands. He yells at Bob as he is still on the floor, looking at the ref. Bob slowly gets up, wondering why the refs didn't call an offensive foul. The hit did not intimidate him but made Bob more determined to play harder. During the second quarter, Abdul and Bob continue to play more physically and trash-talks each other throughout the game.

After considering the possibility of going to jail for fraud and the amount of time he'll probably serve, Joey decides to drive home to explain to his mother about the situation he's in. As he walks into the house, he notices his mom relaxing in her chair, talking on her cell phone. He sits in front of her with both of his elbows on his knees and one hand on each side of his face, looking at her. She continues to talk until she receives the uncomfortable feeling that something is wrong. So she discontinues her phone conversation and asks him sarcastically, "What have you done now?"

Joey takes his hands away from his face and says, "There's something that I have to tell you about me." As she stares at him, he says, "First, I want to say that I love you, and I want to thank you for caring about me the way you do. But I'm not as innocent as you think I am. I have been gambling a lot, and now I've gambled myself into a lot of trouble. I'm the school's treasurer, and I had permission to transfer $50,000 from one bank to another. So two of the basketball players on the team and myself decided to place a $50,000 bet on our school tonight for the state championship game. Then we decided to bet against our school and bet on the other school because we thought the other school had a better chance of winning. We know that the other team is better than us."

His mother nods her head as if she understands what he is saying.

"But when I was going to tell the man who I wanted to bet on, Dad told the man that I wanted to bet on my school, and now I can't get the money back." He takes a deep breath and says, "He just assumed that I was betting on our school and told the man that. So I wanted to know if I could borrow the money from the family bank and somehow pay it back over the years?"

She looks at him with a puzzled face, then smiles at him and says, "I knew you were a gambler. Everybody in the neighborhood knows you're a gambler. What did you think, that I'm stupid or something? All I ever told you was to be careful, that's all. Now, about this money, Joey. Fifty thousand dollars!" She wonders if his gambling habit is worse than she thinks it is. "Don't you think that's a little bit too much? Couldn't you just have given me half of that for all that I've done for you?" she asks jokingly and starts laughing. "So what did your school lose by?"

"I don't know."

"What do you mean you don't know?"

"The game isn't over yet. It just started about a half an hour ago."

"But suppose you win the game? Joey, what are you doing to yourself? Come here." She hits him on the side of his head playfully with her open hand and says, "What'sa matter you? You wanted me to give you $50,000 because you think you might lose? What kind of gambler are you anyway? You even gamble on your bets too." She laughs.

"I tell you, you're weird, but I still love ya. But I'll tell you just like I've told your father. If you lose money on a bet, I won't replace it. If I did, you would gamble that money too. Why don't you wait and see if your school wins? Who knows, they just might win. Why aren't you at the game? You should be there cheering for your school. They might win with a little boost from the students, don't you think?"

"I don't know, Mom, they might, but . . ."

"What are you waiting for? Go win some money for a change and stop crying."

Joey stands up and smiles, then he thanks her for the pep talk and walks out of the house. He thinks positively about his school as he drives to the game. But the closer he gets to the stadium, the more doubt he has about his school winning.

The second quarter begins with West Winsor up by two points, and the pushing and shoving match with the verbal taunting continues with Bob and Abdul. The spectators are enthusiastic about the game as the hollering and screaming intensifies. The game is at a point now where all the players are taunting and criticizing one another, from the floor and from the bench. The passing, dunking, and ballhandling are prodigious.

On one play of the game, Isaiah receives a pass from Bob while running on a fast break toward the basket as Abdul is looking at him, thinking that this short player who is standing at five feet ten inches is going to lay the ball up easily. So Abdul attempts to block his shot in a lackadaisical way but misses the ball as he swings at it. This allows Isaiah to dunk on him. The crowd goes crazy as Abdul is left standing there shocked and embarrassed. He stares at Isaiah in disbelief. Bob hollers at Abdul, "I told you, you ain't got no defense," before running back down the court.

The ref that's paid by the mob from New York is still making false calls on West Winsor and is not giving them any justice. He makes a traveling call on Ace that causes Coach Wynn to jump out of her seat and scream at the referee for making a false call. The ref threatens her with a technical foul if she doesn't sit down and shut up. Another call this referee makes is when the ball is clearly knocked out of bounds by Central. He awards the ball to Central instead of West Winsor. Coach Wynn stands up again, takes her glasses off, and offers them to the referee. He ignores her offer. Joey's father and the mayor look at each other, then look across the floor at the mob from New York, who acknowledge their look and give them a big smile with a thumbs-up sign. The mayor looks back at Joey Senior and shouts to him, "They paid off the head ref! They paid off the head referee!" They look across the floor again and think about their bets.

On the floor, Bob has the ball dribbling toward the basket while Abdul is playing him, shouting, "Who you gonna shoot on, huh? Can you shoot with this defense on you? Can you shoot?"

Bob shoots the ball and shouts at Abdul, "What defense?" as the ball goes in, hitting all net. All of Central's players who heard Bob stop and look at Abdul. Feeling embarrassed and humiliated, Abdul walks up to Bob and pushes him on his chest with both hands, causing Bob to fall down backward. The crowd reacts with boos as security comes on the floor to separate the two players. The referees confer with one another about the assault and are persuaded by the head ref not to kick Abdul out of the game but to sit him on the bench to cool off. Coach Wynn begins to question their decision adamantly, drawing everyone's attention to the matter. The crowd's boos become louder, indicating their disapproval of the ref's decision to keep Abdul in the gym. Coach Wynn threatens all three referees that she is going to sue them for jeopardizing the safety of her students and for allowing the assault to take place. She also threatens them with conspiring and knowingly allowing her students to be abused by Central from all the pushing and shoving that Central initiated. The two refs who weren't bribed feel intimidated by her accusations and threats, so they confer with each other again. As the crowd continues with their boos, the head ref walks over to the security guards and orders them to escort Abdul out of the gym. Central's coach and his players protest by saying, "Bob started it, so he should go too." As Abdul is being escorted off the court, the head referee looks at the mob from New York, then shrugs his shoulders as if to say, "I tried to keep him in the game." When the game resumes, the same ref continues to make false calls on West Winsor. The second quarter ends with West Winsor running their special team offense, which gives them a six-point lead. They're acting as if they won the game already by having the lead at halftime.

While in the locker room, West Winsor is feeling a sense of euphoria for being up by six. When Coach Wynn enters the locker room after them, she picks up a plastic garbage can and throws it against the lockers, almost hitting a player's head. The players are stunned by her actions. The coach hollers at all of them, "Six points, that's all we're up by! They're bums. You should be blowing them out by at least twenty points. They tried to intimidate you. It looks as if they did intimidate you by the way you're playing. The special play is not working because you're not making it work."

Bayshawn interrupts her and says, "The special play is working. That's why we're winning by six points."

"Shut up while I'm talking!" she shouts back. "I want the defense taking the ball from them and reading their passes every time they dribble the ball. And if you can't do that, I'll get somebody in there that can get the job done. You guys are playing as if someone told you that y'all can't beat Central. Out of all the practices and games we had, this is the only game that counts. This is do or die. But it's up to you now. Central is either going to make you or break you. And the whole state is watching to see if you fall like the rest because they think you can't beat Central. So it's up to you to prove them wrong. I've done all I could to get you here. Now it's up to you." She wags her head, turns, and walks out of the locker room, leaving the team in a state of confusion, knowing that they have done the best that they can do.

While she's gone, Bayshawn looks at Ace and asks, "What's up with her? She acts like we're losing the game. We're beating the best team in the state, and she don't even appreciate it. What's up with that, Ace? How do you satisfy a woman?"

Ace looks at him and asks, "Why are you asking me?"

Bayshawn takes a few steps forward while thinking about the money from the bet they made, knowing that they should be losing. He tells the players as if he suddenly has this great idea, "Well, if she don't appreciate us winning, then maybe we should lose the game."

All the players look at him as if he's crazy, except Ace, who smiles, gets up, and shakes his head and walks out of the locker room.

During the third quarter, Central takes the lead by five points. The head ref is still cheating for Central. On one play, the ref makes a false walking call on Bayshawn while standing in front of a group of West Winsor High students. The student who borrowed a book from the library while looking for Joey has the book with him at the game, as if he really kept his promise to the old librarian to read the book. But in reality, he wants to give the book to the librarian after he heard that she is going to be there sitting with the team. After the ref makes the false call, the crowd boos him again. The boy who has the book throws it on the floor in front of the head referee, landing it at his feet. The ref becomes indignant as he picks the book up and reads the cover, with the title *How the Game of Basketball Is Played.* Then he rips the paperback book in half and throws it on the side of the ball court. The old librarian, who realizes that it is one of her books, approaches the ref and grabs his ear. When the ref pushes her away, the boy who threw the book runs onto the floor and punches the referee in the mouth. Security grabs him and escorts him out of the gym. The crowd applauds the boy's actions as he is being escorted out. With a busted and bleeding lip, the ref can no longer officiate the game. So he also leaves to receive medical attention. The crowd applauds that too.

Joey Senior and the mayor look over at the mob from New York and smile at them while applauding. The New York mobsters frown back at them when Joey's father gives one of his runners some money to give to the boy for the assault. The runner leaves the stands and goes out in the direction of the guards as they are escorting the boy out.

When the game resumes, Coach Wynn decides to make an all-out blitz on Central, which is making her team tired. Her other strategy is working by confusing her opponent's team. Her all-out strategy is do or die, even if she has to sacrifice a player's life. She thinks about the odds that are against her and now that her obstacles are out of the way, she is going straight up and attacking her enemies with a vengeance. Every chance she gets to make a substitution for those who are tired, Coach Wynn does it without hesitation. Her intuition about the game is if a referee can be paid off, then so can a player.

CHAPTER 7

When the third quarter ended, West Winsor is winning by seven points. Bayshawn and Isaiah complain to the coach about how exhausted they are. They are willing to continue if they can get a little rest. Coach Wynn sits them on the bench for a few minutes during the start of the fourth quarter, telling the rest of the players that if they hold on for this last quarter, the game is theirs.

"We've come too far to lose now. All we need is eight more minutes—that's all, eight more minutes," she says desperately as if their lives depended on it. "Your resilience to their defense pressure is paying off for us," she states as she clinches her fist while shaking it.

As the fourth quarter begins, Joey enters the parking lot. On the court, the special defense proves to be very effective (again) because the five defensive players are lined up in the middle of the court with a gap between them, double-teaming and sometimes triple-teaming Central to steal the ball away from them.

Joey uses his team pass to get into the sold-out game and sits away from the team, still feeling ashamed of his father's decision to bet on his team. Joey doesn't know who's winning at this time because the score only shows Home and Guest on the scoreboard. But he's curious about who the home team is. Joey assumes that the home team is Central because the home team's score is leading by twelve points. Two minutes of playing time go by when Joey notices something that he thought was strange taking place on the scoreboard. Every time West Winsor scored, the number changed on the home side, which had the lead.

West Winsor scores again and again to the extent that they have an eighteen-point lead. Joey tells a spectator sitting next to him that they're giving Central's points to West Winsor. When Central scores, he tells the guy, "See. You see that? They're giving the wrong score." When the dude tells Joey that the score is right, Joey responds with amazement, "West Winsor's winning?"

"Yeah, we're winning. We've been winning all game. Where you been at?" Joey jumps up with excitement, runs down the steps, and goes over to his team. Central calls for a time-out to stop the special defense run-and-gun show that West Winsor is using against them, which is hurting Central.

On the way to the bench, with five minutes left to play, Bayshawn stops Ace and asks him, "Should we start losing now?"

Ace tells him, "We can win this, yo. Look at the score."

"Yeah, Ace. But we can't win no money."

While Ace is walking toward the bench looking disgusted, he tells Bayshawn, "You're right. You know what we got to do, so let's do it."

Ace and Bayshawn's plan is to control the ball and lose it, then miss every shot they take so that Central can get the ball and score. By doing this, Central can catch up and pass them on points. They also plan on letting Central players score on them when they play their men on defense. During the time-out, Joey runs over to his team with excitement and says, "I bet on us. I bet on y'all, and we're winning."

Isaiah asks him, "Where you been at, yo? We needed some fresh towels. How you going to be the manager when you can't get here on time for some towels?"

Bayshawn hollers at Joey, "Yo, you said that you were gonna bet on—"

Before he can finish, Ace interrupts him and says, "If he said he betted on us, then he made the right choice."

The horn blows, indicating that the time-out has expired. Coach Wynn comes over to see what all the commotion is about. She looks at Joey and says, "Glad that you could finally make it." The team ignores the horn and their coach and continues to talk.

Bob tells Joey, "You should have stayed where you were because we don't need you. See, I told y'all we didn't need him."

Joey continues by saying, "I put all of the money on us, and we're winning."

Coach Wynn tells the team, "All right, team, let's go. It's time. The refs are waiting."

The horn sounds, and the ref blows his whistle again. Coach Wynn hollers at her players to get on the floor. Bayshawn asks Joey, "Why did you bet on us? Why you ain't tell somebody you bet on us?" The horn blows again, and the ref comes over to the team and warns them that if they don't come out on the floor, he will give them a technical. Central's coach runs over to the refs as he shouts at them, "Tech, tech, give them a technical! If that was my team, you would be giving me a tech."

West Winsor's players slowly walk on to the floor. While walking, Bayshawn tells Ace, "If we win this, we could get paid, yo. You heard what he said."

"Yeah, I heard him, he put all the money on us."

"So, Ace, should we just slow it down and let the time expire?"

"No, Bayshawn. Let's make a statement to them. Let's blow them out." With that, Bayshawn smiles.

The game resumes with less than five minutes to play. Bayshawn and Ace are enthusiastic to win now, so they play much harder and encourage the rest of the team to play a little harder also. West Winsor's style of playing frustrates Central to the point where Central can't pass the ball effectively without getting it stolen. On one play, when Central's player takes the ball out of bounds after West Winsor scores, the Central player throws the ball inbounds out of frustration, not paying attention to whom he was throwing the ball to. This gave Ace the opportunity to grab the ball and score again.

West Winsor is up by twenty-three points before Central calls for another time-out. Central's coach calls for the time-out so that his team can regroup to calm down and organize themselves and stop arguing with one another. He knows that Central's defeat is imminent.

With two minutes remaining in the game, Joey is on the sideline, running up and down the court, going crazy, thinking about the money he'd won. He also encourages the team to play even harder to ensure that they have a definite win. Joey waves to his father, knowing that they're both winners. It was not until one minute left in the game that Coach Wynn takes Bob, Bayshawn, Isaiah, Squib, and Ace out of the game and puts in the other players. The crowd gives them a standing ovation, recognizing them to be the best high school team in the state of New Jersey.

With less than a minute to play, the rest of the team stands on their feet and watches the rest of the game until the time expires. When the game is over, the crowd erupts! West Winsor's team goes over to Central's players, shakes their hands, congratulates them, and thanks them for a good game. The spectators continue to applaud to show their appreciation to the winners and the losers as well.

During the next day, all the newspapers are forced to print the game on their front pages. Coach Wynn complains to the news media that they were biased against her because she is a woman coaching a boys' basketball team. She also complains that she had to use a billboard just to get the recognition she deserves for coaching the team. The news media promise to make it up to her by giving her headline news with the first three pages dedicated to West Winsor High School and its basketball team.

The following Monday morning, Ace drives Fran'Sheila to school in a new black 765 BMW. Bayshawn is behind him, driving a black Jaguar with the music banging. They bought these cars over the weekend from the gambling proceeds. Ace sees Abdul talking with his boys as they sit on the steps in front of Central High School. He gets out of his car with Bayshawn following him to discuss the game with the fellas. After they greet one another, Abdul tells them, "I see that y'all living the good life now. So does this mean that y'all going to forget about us?"

Ace tells him, "We wouldn't be here if we did. And it's all good. You got them big college scouts feeling you,

Abdul. I hope you don't forget about us when you make the pros."

Bayshawn tells him, "Work on your attitude, and stop punching people. The pros look at that too. It ain't all about playing ball. It's about attitude, yo."

"What? You're my big brother now, Bayshawn?"

"Naw, I'm just being constructive, that's all."

"We could have won that game if I didn't get kicked out. You know that, right?"

Bayshawn smiles at Abdul and says, "Sure, you right."

Ace says to them, "We gotta bounce."

They shake hands and give one another half hugs before agreeing to meet after school.

That same morning, Joey uses some of the proceeds from the bet for investments and deposits the $50,000 back into the bank that the School Board of Education does business with. He considers the $50,000 as a no-interest loan. That's why he borrowed the money under false pretense.

After buying a car, Ace invests his money in savings bonds and stashes money away for college.

Two months after their high school graduation, Ace, Isaiah, and Bayshawn decide to celebrate Isaiah's departure for his enrollment into the US Military. Bayshawn has started a business selling clothes as a street vender on the blocks in Harlem, New York. Ace is going his way to Morehouse College in Georgia. Their friendship will still exist, but it would be from a distance.

Before transferring to West Windsor High School, Ace gave serious thoughts about enrolling into Morehouse College in the state of Georgia. His decision is based on the economic growth and the job opportunities the state has to offer. This idea encourages his family also to move to Georgia to challenge the country atmosphere. This move will allow his studies to be uninterrupted by the street thugs, or his boys, who grew up with him, wilding out on the streets of the Wilbur section in Trenton, New Jersey. Just the thought of him graduating from college is exciting to Ace and his family.

One late Sunday night, Ace celebrates the anticipated move with the fellas, drinking at a nearby lounge. The drinking lasts into the early hours of Monday morning. Ace, Isaiah, and Bayshawn stumble into Isaiah's sister's house at three o'clock on Monday morning. She isn't home at the time. Isaiah's sister is on a bus excursion with her neighborhood friends. Bayshawn lays on the couch in the living room to sleep off his hangover, and Isaiah goes upstairs to his room. Ace goes upstairs and walks into the bedroom that is farther down the hall, which is Isaiah's sister Leticia's room. Her room is overwhelmed with the fresh scent of potpourri aroma and a slight French perfume fragrance. With the aroma of the potpourri and perfume smell together, this combination will allow your dreams to be more pleasant.

The early-morning feeling of nausea and stomach cramps that feel like kicks, with the combination of headaches, once again awakens Fran'Sheila. This morning's wake-up experience started three weeks ago and continues to get worse each day. Her remedy for this discomfort is the normal over-the-counter drugs for stomach pain that seem to temporarily work. Her solution to avoid vomiting in the mornings is to abstain from eating foods after 6:00 p.m. But as she reflected upon it, the vomit occurs at any time of the day. The theory that mother knows best does have a sense of validity to it. *Maybe a homemade remedy could be the solution,* is her thought to this discomfort.

After getting dressed, she approaches her mother with her hands on her upper abdomen. Fran'Sheila talks to her about the fry-cooked foods that her mom makes.

"Mom, I'm going to have to eat more baked foods until this stomach virus goes away. It feels like it's getting worse each time I wake up. I'm starting to vomit all of the time. My headaches just stay with me each morning. I'm always fatigued, then I get hot for no reason at all. I think it's the seasoning that you put in the food."

Fran'Sheila's mother looks at her with much concern and says, "There's nothing wrong with my stomach. I eat the same foods that you eat in here. It's probably the fast food from the streets you had yesterday."

"No, it's not that. It's your food, Mom," Fran'Sheila shouts back. "It must be the grease in the food, and it's also interfering with my monthly cycle too. I haven't had one in three months. I might just need to be a vegetarian."

Her mother's mouth opens without saying a word. She covers her mouth with both of her hands and slowly shakes her head from side to side. Fran'Sheila slightly closes her eyes as she looks at her mother, as if her mother forgot to tell her about the new seasoning that was put into the collard greens. After her mother takes her hands off her face, she puts both her hands on Fran'Sheila's shoulders. She takes a deep breath, looks Fran'Sheila in her eyes, and says, "You're pregnant!"

Fran'Sheila's words are lost for a response. But when she finally finds something to say to her mother, the "mother knows best" concept has changed. She changes this concept so that she can try to justify her next words, trying to convince her mom that she's wrong.

For eighteen years, the good-girl image has made a positive impression with her mother. She is concerned that her deviate lifestyle might become exposed by being pregnant.

"It don't mean that I'm pregnant just because I'm feeling sick." Fran'Sheila says this as if she graduated from medical school. "Anybody could feel like this. It's just a stomach virus or . . ." She pauses to carefully look at her mother's face. Her mother looks at Fran'Sheila as if to say, "I've experienced that feeling before when I was pregnant with you." Fran'Sheila's mother is a devout Christian. Usually, whenever there is a discussion pertaining to life, her mother always quotes scriptures to resolve the issue. So Fran'Sheila patiently waits for the criticism and the ostracism from her mom. But this time, she admonishes Fran'Sheila by saying, "That's between you and Jehovah God, but I'll be here for you when you need me."

With her mom's words of admonishment in her heart, Fran'Sheila, for a few seconds, is hoping that her pregnancy is divine. Hopefully, the way Jesus was born. Knowing that the only human being that could have impregnated her was Ace. Telling Ace this exciting news is going to be difficult because of his enrollment in college. Or maybe a child might give Ace a little more initiative to succeed in college, she thinks as she walks out of her home to go to the store.

The Monday morning adrenaline pushes Isaiah out of his bed, through the house, and out of the front door. Time is against Isaiah due to oversleeping with a hangover. At 7:30 a.m., Isaiah is usually at his fast-food restaurant job, punching his card into the time slot. But this morning is the post-going-away celebration, so here is another excuse for being late the boss must hear.

"Bayshawn, wake up and pick this trash up before my sister comes home!" Isaiah snaps as he aggressively pushes Bayshawn's shoulder before heading out the door. Ace was nowhere in sight this morning as he lay in Leticia's bed wrapped under pillows, blankets, clothes, and sheets. This depicts the way her bed was left after Leticia's departure from her house as she rushed to join her friends for the weekend bus excursion. While Isaiah is walking out of the house, he notices Leticia walking toward him with a leather suitcase in her hand. She complains about how she is going to be late for work and needs a ride.

"Isaiah, I'm going to take a quick shower and throw on some clothes and ride with you, okay?"

"I'm running late myself. Bayshawn is getting ready to go too! He's down stairs," Isaiah responds as he rushes to his car. Leticia despises Bayshawn because he rejected her proposition for him to be her man after her other man, Rock, passed away from a drive-by. Rock used to supply her with the finer things in life and perpetuated her diva status in the hood with designer clothes.

Bayshawn knows that she is a manipulator and a hustler who is heartless. He also knows that she's hating on him because he's not pushing her around in his Jaguar car, which is her favorite dream car. She walks into the house and begins to bark at him. "I know you got somewhere else to go this morning. If not, you still got to get up and get out of my house." She loves to demonstrate to him verbally her hate toward him. But because of the time, Leticia runs upstairs into her bedroom where Ace is buried underneath clothes and covers. Unaware of his presence, she takes off her clothes as she stands on the other side of the bed, grabs her towel, and heads for the shower down the hall.

Bayshawn goes to the bathroom downstairs to freshen up before going home. His drinking hangover makes him want to hibernate. He definitely doesn't feel like getting up. After leaving the bathroom, he decides to lie on the couch just for a few more minutes of sleep.

While on the road, Isaiah stops at the local convenience store for coffee. This antidote usually helps cure his hangover in the mornings with a small bag of peanuts. As he leaves the store with his goods, Fran'Sheila walks up to his car. She recognizes him as he enters his car and begins to start the engine. She waves at him to speak.

"Running late this morning?" she says with a bright smile.

"I'm usually on time, but I'll get there," he responds. He begins to pull off when he shouts, "Hey, Ace and Bayshawn spent the night at my house, in case you tried to call him. Deuces." Then he pulls off.

Time isn't on Bayshawn's mind as he lies on the couch to get his thoughts together. Ace is still buried under the sheets and clothes that are on the bed. Fran'Sheila buys some medication for her stomach pain and heads to Isaiah's house, which is two blocks up the street. As she walks, Fran'Sheila is trying to find the words to express this exciting news to Ace about his first child. At this time, Leticia has left the bathroom, finishing taking a shower. Leticia enters her room with a towel wrapped around her body and heads for the radio at the end of the bed, which Ace is sleeping on. After turning on the radio, the sound of R&B music is heard throughout the house. As she turns toward the bed, Leticia notices a pair of sneakers, pants, underwear, socks, and shirt on the side of the floor. At the same time, the covers on the top of the bed start to move. She doesn't know if she should run out of the room or if this was one of those girls Bayshawn or her brother Isaiah had over the house last night. Leticia sees a body emerging from under the clothes and sheets on the bed. She takes two steps back and grabs the biggest can of hair spray that is on the dresser to throw at whatever is coming from under those sheets. Ace throws the linens off him in a bit of rage for the one who disturbed his peaceful dream. He stares at Leticia as if he could kill her with his eyes. Leticia doesn't mind having Ace in her bed but not under these circumstances. Ace is the kind of dude that she has to have but doesn't want to holla at him because she wants to be pursued.

"What you doing here, lady? How'd you get up in here?"

"What? Excuse me, but this is my house," she says with her left hand on her hip with an attitude.

"This is what?" he says as he looks around the room, realizing it isn't his room. "Oh. How I . . . What time is it?" he asks, squinting his eyes, trying to avoid the light.

"It's late, and I'm late. But you can come back later if you're not too busy with your girlfriend," Leticia says while looking at Ace's chest as he moves to sit on the side of the bed, covering his waist and legs the best he can with the sheets. Ace ignores her offer while trying to figure out how he got there and what he did while he was there all night.

"I'm running late for work. Tell Bayshawn to get out of my house if he didn't leave yet."

Fran'Sheila walks up to the front porch to look inside the house through the screen door. Fran'Sheila sees Bayshawn lying on the couch on his back and decides to walk in through the unlocked door. Isaiah told her about Bayshawn and Ace being at his house, but all she sees is Bayshawn as she glances through the dining room and kitchen. She doesn't want to awake Bayshawn, so she goes upstairs. Bayshawn faintly sees the back of her as she walks up the steps before he gets up to leave. Fran'Sheila reaches the top of the steps, not knowing where Ace is sleeping, so she walks toward the room where the music is coming from.

"That music is too loud. It got my head banging. Can you turn the volume down on that, please?" Ace states to Leticia. As Leticia turns the volume down on the radio, Fran'Sheila walks into the room where she recognize Ace's voice, with a big smile on her face, thinking about her unborn child. Her euphoria changes to pain as she observes Ace sitting on the side of the bed with his back and backside exposed while Leticia stands at the foot of bed.

Fran'Sheila opens her mouth to speak, but she is too shocked and confused to articulate. Leticia's first impression at seeing Fran'Sheila is that Fran'Sheila spent the night at her house with Ace. But the look on Fran'Sheila's face reveals that she is shocked to see him in her bed. Leticia doesn't say a word but allows Fran'Sheila to speak. Ace is surprised to see her too! But he knows somehow he is going to get the blame for all this. Leticia still has the can of hair spray in her hand while trying to hold the short towel in place so it remains closed. She tries to at least appear decent.

"What's going on here, Ace? Why are your clothes off? Why you in her bed?" she asks but already speculates about what had already happened. "I don't know. I just got up," he says sarcastically while trying not to answer too many questions. His sarcasm does not help his case in this matter but enrages her emotions.

"You've been in her bed all night?" She looks at Leticia for an answer as to what they were doing in her room all night.

"I think you and your man need to discuss this outside because I'm running late for work."

"No," Fran'Sheila snaps back. "We're going to discuss this now. You always wanted to holla at him, and the first opportunity you got to be with him, you took it."

Leticia always showed her hate for Fran'Sheila in the streets, and Fran'Sheila didn't have any love for Leticia either. Leticia never interfered when her former man, Rock, disrespected Fran'Sheila out in public. She condoned his insults to Fran'Sheila and at times participated in the insults. Leticia knows she is right but is wrong about the opportunity because she didn't holla at him to get Ace in her bed.

Leticia feels irate as Fran'Sheila stands in her bedroom, telling her how she got with her man.

"You could believe whatever you want to, I'm not going to argue with you," Leticia says as she shakes her head from side to side while gripping the can tightly.

Ace was too drunk to remember anything. The loud music doesn't help his memory either. At this time, he barely can remember his name. Ace tries reaching for his pants and at the same time holding the covers on his upper legs. The bending over causes severe pain in his head. The morning hangover is interfering with his thoughts and movements. Ace doesn't feel like talking. He just wants to go back to sleep. Fran'Sheila turns and walks out of the room, emotionally hurt and destroyed. Ace calls out to her with no response. Leticia walks into the closet to look for her clothes. At the same time, Ace grabs and throws on whatever clothes he can and rushes out of the room after Fran'Sheila.

By the end of the day, the word on the street is that Ace got busted in Leticia's bed, butt naked, by his woman. The other talk is that Leticia took Fran'Sheila's man, and he spent the night over at her house in her bed. Isaiah hears about the talk on the street, but at the time, he doesn't know that Ace was in her room and doesn't know how long Ace stayed there after he went to work. Bayshawn didn't see or hear the commotion because, after Fran'Sheila walked upstairs, he left the house.

Although time is supposed to heal all wounds, Fran'Sheila's hurt is too deep. Her thoughts are on her rejection of Leticia's former man Rock's proposition to spend time with her and Ace's acceptance of Leticia's proposition for Ace to be in Leticia's bed. Sleeping with the enemy is not acceptable to Fran'Sheila. She warned him in the past not to disrespect her with any of her enemies.

Ace and his family are scheduled to fly to Georgia to live there. Moorehouse College is his choice to attend, and his family's choice is to live in Georgia too. Ace would have had a change of plans if he knew about his son.

While in Georgia, Ace continues to attempt to contact Fran'Sheila but to no avail. She changed her phone numbers and refuses to write him back. His dilemma is to try to explain to her about what happened that morning without his knowing what happened. After discussing with Bayshawn about that ordeal and trying to put different times together, there still was no conclusion.

Leticia knows the truth but decides to see how much Fran'Sheila trusts Ace. She feels that if Fran'Sheila doesn't trust and believe in Ace, then he shouldn't be with her.

Isaiah continues to follow his dream and enrolls into the US Navy, so he cannot be reached. As time goes on, Leticia never agrees to the rumors about her sleeping with Ace but her acquiescence allows people to believe that the rumors are true. When she sees Fran'Sheila out in public, she would smile at her as if something really did happen that morning in her bed.

Ace knows that the love Fran'Sheila has for him is gone when his letters are not answered and her phone numbers to her home and cell are changed. He is hurt but doesn't feel guilty about that morning because he doesn't feel as though he did anything wrong. But the problem is explaining how and why he was in a woman's bed, naked, with the woman standing next to him wrapped only in a towel. He came to the same conclusion that maybe something did happen, and the alcohol just got the best of him.

About a year later, Leticia gets the opportunity to discuss the matter with Fran'Sheila after her mother's funeral. Fran'Sheila's mother died unexpectedly. This causes more hardship for Fran'Sheila. The discussion is intense but basically unilateral with Leticia doing all the talking. Although Leticia has a treacherous heart, her heart goes out to Fran'Sheila, knowing that she has no other living family member nearby. Fran'Sheila has a two-month-old baby boy with no man to support her, all because of a misunderstanding. These two factors play a major part in her decision to talk and to clear up the misunderstanding. Under the circumstances that Fran'Sheila is in, Leticia decides to give some comfort to a girl that seems to be losing those that she loves. She finally sees Fran'Sheila strolling her baby near Faircrest Park. Fran'Sheila attempts to ignore her as Leticia approaches.

"Hello," Leticia blurts out as she approaches her. But Fran'Sheila continues to walk without saying a word. "I need to talk to you about the—"

"You need to leave me alone," Fran'Sheila snaps back at her. "And that's what you better do." Fran'Sheila continues to push the stroller as Leticia walks behind her, trying not to provoke her. Fran'Sheila realizes that her warning did not convince Leticia to stop talking to her. So Fran'Sheila turns toward Leticia and balls up her fist as she steps to her while biting down on her bottom lip.

"Look, I don't want to argue or fight with you, but if we have to fight, then I'll just talk as we fight." Leticia made this statement while slowly walking backward, away from Fran'Sheila. Leticia is five years older than Fran'Sheila, so she decides to be the mature and level-headed adult in this. "I never told anybody about Ace being in my bed. And apparently, you never talked to him about it. From what I was told, he was too drunk to remember how he got into my bed. I came home as Isaiah was leaving to go to work, and that was a few minutes before he saw you at the store."

Fran'Sheila decides to listen because, at that time, she never did get an explanation for what she saw and always knew that she might have overreacted. She wished that it was a misunderstanding, but her pride and anger led her to speculate from what she saw.

Leticia continues, "I saw Bayshawn downstairs. He saw me when I came in. He knows how long I've been upstairs. Bayshawn knew that I was in a hurry when I ran upstairs. I told my brother that I was running late and that I needed a ride. When I got upstairs, I didn't see Ace on my bed. He was underneath the covers. You've seen all of the clothes and sheets on my bed. All I did was run in my room, get undressed, and run in the shower. When I got out of the shower, I turned on the radio, and that's when the bed started to move. Then I saw someone coming out from underneath my bed covers. I still had my towel on me, so he ain't seen nothing."

Fran'Sheila feels a little relieved by that statement.

"When those covers started to move, I grabbed my spray can and was ready to hit whoever was coming from out of that bed. You saw the can in my hand."

Fran'Sheila reflects on the incident without committing.

"I was scared and confused. That's when you came into the room. I didn't know what was going on, you didn't know what was going on, and Ace didn't know what was happening."

Leticia starts to laugh when she says, "When he came from underneath that cover, he asked me what I was doing in his bedroom. I had to let him know quick that he was in my house. He got it all twisted. Ace looked around my room while lying on the bed and realized that he wasn't home. I didn't say too much to you then because I didn't like the fact that you were in my room too. I thought that you spent the night in my house."

Fran'Sheila feels at ease to respond and to apologize without apologizing, knowing that no intimacy occurred that night between those two. Fran'Sheila explains to Leticia why she was in her house. "Isaiah told me at the store that Ace was at your house. When I got there, the door was open, and I saw Bayshawn on the couch, so I walked in. I heard you were away on a bus trip, so I went upstairs where the music was playing, looking for Ace. When I heard his voice, I walked into your room. But when I saw you standing there, it didn't look right. It didn't look right at all," Fran'Sheila says carefully, trying not to put the blame on anyone.

Leticia tells her, "Even if you would have asked him about that day, he was too drunk that night to remember to tell you because it was like missing pieces to a puzzle. So everybody had to have been there together to get an understanding of it all. I talked to my brother about it. He said he didn't see Ace in the house that morning. He thought Ace got up early and went home before he got up. But my brother did talk to Bayshawn before he went to work. Isaiah laughed at the situation when I told him. Have you talked to Ace about that morning?"

Fran'Sheila tries to find an easy way to respond to that question, knowing that she didn't allow Ace to give her an explanation. "I haven't talked to Ace since the bedroom incident. It's been over a year since we've talked."

Leticia glances at the baby and says, "Your son is very cute. What's his name?"

"Diamond. He's Ace's first child," Fran'Sheila tells her as she picks up her baby from the carriage and smiles.

"Does Ace know that he has a son?"

Fran'Sheila takes a deep breath, knowing now that the bed incident was all a misunderstanding. She puts her face toward the ground and wags her head from side to side.

"I wanted to tell him that morning, but it didn't work out right. When he called me, I didn't answer his calls, then I got my phone number changed, and that was that. He probably got disgusted with me and gave up on me before moving to Georgia. He's stubborn like that!"

"I know that's right. But maybe he'll come back to Trenton before his classes start to visit some friends or something," Leticia tells her as she tries to be optimistic.

Fran'Sheila smiles a little and says, "I hope so because I owe him an apology and a big hug."

"Hey, I got to go, Fran'Sheila. You still mad at me?"

Fran'Sheila smiles and says, "No, my bad. I overreacted. I apologize."

After hugging, they part as friends with a better understanding about the whole ordeal and about each other. The only scenario that Fran'Sheila is facing now is talking to Ace.

CHAPTER 8

College life seems to agree with Ace. The academic course allows him to discipline himself with the challenge of completing all his work assignments. There are no distractions from family or friends. Although his nearest friends are hundreds of miles away, the feeling of being homesick affects him to some degree. During his first semester, his grade average is way up, and he feels content with himself and what he has accomplished thus far. This is good knowledge to Ace's family, but he wants his friends to have a share in his happiness and success.

On Saturday morning, Ace takes time out from his busiest homework schedule to find out the happenings in the hood in Trenton, New Jersey. Ace calls Bayshawn with no success. His calls to Leticia's house to ask about Isaiah and when he's coming back home from the navy, was shocking and intense.

"Hello, Leticia, this is Ace. What's good? When is Isaiah coming home? Has he called or wrote to you anything? When was the last time you talked to him? Has he asked about me? How can I get in touch with him?" he asks with such excitement. Leticia is reluctant to answer because of his disregard for her well-being. Ace is elated to talk to somebody from home; he didn't even have the courtesy to ask her how she was doing. Leticia feels disrespected by Ace not even asking her about the bedroom incident or even apologizing for being in her bed. So after a brief pause from the questions, Ace continues, "Hello, hello, Leticia, can you hear me?"

"Yes, I'm here, Ace. How you doing?"

"I'm all right, lady. I'm just down here trying to get educated that's all."

"Ace, you haven't talked to me in over a year, and you can't even ask me how I'm doing or how I've been doing? This is my phone and my house you're calling. I guess I don't matter or don't even count, do I? It seems like you went to college and just got stupid, ignorant, and disrespectful. The last time I talked to you, you were in my bedroom. You didn't even have the respect to even thank me for a wonderful time in my bed. You didn't call me or nothing after you spent the night in my bed. You're selfish and ignorant just like the rest of your friends. Since you got twenty-one questions, let me ask you a couple. When was the last time you talked to your girlfriend?"

Ace thinks about Fran'Sheila, knowing that is one of his next questions he is going to ask her. "I was going to ask you about her. I haven't heard from her since we left your house last year."

"So that's how you do women. Love them and leave them, huh?"

"No, I wasn't with her that night or that morning."

"Oh yeah, that's right. You were in my bed that morning." Those words bring back unanswered questions. "Well, I talked to her last month, and our conversation was about you and me."

Ace becomes nervous and begins to sweat a little. He's wondering what she told Fran'Sheila about his overnight stay that would discourage Fran'Sheila not to call him.

"What is your address, Ace? Maybe I'll ask Fran'Sheila to write you a letter or something."

Ace gives Leticia his cell phone number and his address with the assumption that Leticia and he were intimate with each other that night. "Well, since we're on this level of being inconsiderate," Leticia says softly, "I'll be the first to inform you that you have a three-month-old son. His name is Diamond."

Those words hit him like a hard right hook. It leaves him speechless and cold. Now his thoughts have been confirmed.

"I'll drive him down to you. He looks just like you, Ace. When is the best day to come down?"

"The best day would be on a Monday. But why do it? Or why he has to be mine? You know we have to be sure about this."

"Ace, once you see this boy, you won't be asking these questions. If you want a blood test, those things are possible too. I'll be down soon, so you can see what a wonderful child you brought into this world. I'll be down in a couple of weeks. I'll kiss the baby for you. Bye, Daddy."

With these words, she hangs up the phone. Ace holds on to the phone after she hangs up. He shakes his head from side to side, feeling disgusted. His mother walks by him and asks, "Is there something wrong?' She thinks that Ace's phone call has something to do with their move to Georgia.

"No, Mom, there's nothing wrong. I just can't get in touch with my friends, that's all." The only thoughts that were on Ace's mind before this conversation were on his education. Now he has entered a new phenomenon of the baby-momma drama. Money is no issue for providing for his son. The problem is that Ace has no love for Leticia.

Ace is hoping that this all could be a mistake. He isn't feeling Leticia, and he has no recollection of copulations with her. Ace begins to induce self-hatred for becoming a father out of wedlock, especially with a woman that he has no feelings for. The woman that he is feeling kicked him to the curb. Now, it would be very difficult for him to explain to Fran'Sheila that he wasn't feeling Leticia the night he slept in her bed after he produced a child with her. This drama affects his schoolwork and his daily activities. After many attempts to contact Bayshawn, he finally gets in touch with him by phone. They have a long conversation about everything. But Ace is skeptical about telling him about his baby with Bayshawn's enemy. So he prolongs the conversation to see if Bayshawn knows anything about it or what he knows about anything.

"Hey, have you seen Fran'Sheila out there, yo?"

"Naw, I've been in New York on the grind, selling clothes and getting paid in Harlem."

Ace becomes more impatient with him. "I've heard Leticia had a baby. Have you seen her? Who's the baby's father? What's the word on the street?"

Bayshawn laughs and says, "The word on the street is that Leticia stole Fran'Sheila's man. That's the word on the street." After thinking about it, Bayshawn asks, "Ace, did you get Leticia pregnant?"

Ace refuses to answer him, so Bayshawn tells him, "I didn't think you were into that."

"I'm not into that," Ace says.

"Well, you where into that if you got her pregnant."

"Whatever," Ace replies. Bayshawn laughs at him again and says, "The baby's not mine, and that's all that matters. I think I saw Fran'Sheila babysitting somebody's baby a couple of days ago when I drove by her house."

"Did she ask about me?"

"I didn't get a chance to talk to her. She didn't see me as I drove by, Ace. Hey! I got to bounce. Ace, is this your cell number on my phone?"

"Yeah, that's me, Bayshawn. Put my name on that and don't lose it."

"All right, I'll holla, Ace. Peace."

Ace is still puzzled and worried.

That Friday, Leticia talked to Fran'Sheila and convinced her to take the long journey to Atlanta, Georgia, to visit Ace with her. Leticia wants to ease his worries about his prodigy. She anticipates how shocked and surprised he will be to know that Fran'Sheila is really his baby's momma. Leticia decides to keep the suspense about the mother of Ace's son a secret until they arrive in Georgia, and finally, the truth will be told. Leticia still has feelings for Ace, but even if she is to get involved with him, there's still the baby-momma drama with his ex. But Ace isn't feeling her like that. Fran'Sheila and Leticia decide on the day and time to get on the road to Georgia. Leticia informs Ace when she will be leaving New Jersey and when he should expect her and Diamond to arrive. The long ride will commence in a rent-a-car. Euphoria sets in with Fran'Sheila. She can finally introduce her son to his daddy and hopefully bond with him so that they can be one happy family. Leticia just wants to throw this in Ace's face, that she is the mother by being facetious, and then go shopping in downtown Atlanta, Georgia. She knows that the suspense is killing him, thinking that Leticia produced his son. This is an opportunity for her to clear her name and make him see what might have been. To Leticia, maybe if he contemplates about it, he might just want to have a child with her. But just the thrill of making him worry and sweat is satisfying to her.

The thought of seeing her first love again is overwhelming for Fran'Sheila. She packed for the weekend trip as if she is moving in with Ace. The road trip began early Sunday morning at 6:00 a.m. The ride is not the least boring as Fran'Sheila tells her whole life story. She articulates about how Ace would be proud to have a son, especially since it is his firstborn and only child. Fran'Sheila states how Ace wants to finish college first and get married, then have four kids. "Ace said that he will be there for his child and family financially so they wouldn't have to struggle to remain solvent."

The excitement got the best of her with her newfound friend Leticia. In hopes that their conversation would remain just between themselves, Fran'Sheila exposes all of Ace's finances. The high school gambling bet, the investments in the stock market with Joey, and the buying of $60,000 in US savings bonds are spoken of too. She tells Leticia how Ace's dealings with Joey involves the mafia and big money bankers with Joey's father and his father's friends. Ace's plans to set up computer software sales and engage in insider trading in the stock market so that they would know when to sell and when to trade. She let it be known that Ace will be getting crazy pay, but he can't start spending too much of the money at once.

"He might get too much attention. That's why he had to move from Trenton, New Jersey," Fran'Sheila tells her. The conversation goes throughout the morning, into the afternoon and evening hours. Fran'Sheila changes the topic for conversation from Ace and talks about herself. "I'm going to be his queen and going to be living larger than life. Ace said whoever he marries, they wouldn't have to ever work again. He said all they had to do was to stay at home and be there for him and his child. I can buy anything I want, travel anywhere I want to travel, and just be happy for the rest of my life, raising our son. I'll introduce the baby to him first. I know he is excited about seeing his son."

Fran'Sheila laughs while saying, "He's going to be like, 'What the . . . ' when he sees me carrying Diamond toward him, all the while knowing that Diamond is your son. He's not going to know what to think. But I am going to apologize to him about the way I acted when I had a lack of trust in him." Fran'Sheila looks back at her son, Diamond, who is sitting in the baby's seat behind the driver's seat, and smiles at him.

"I'm making sure his seat belt is still on. Just in case we have an accident, he won't fall out of his seat," Fran'Sheila states while still smiling. As Leticia's thoughts are on her shopping spree and nighttime partying in downtown Atlanta, Georgia, she envisions herself being in Fran'Sheila's position of being financially secure with Ace.

While driving, Leticia thinks about who is going to reimburse her for the time and effort she is spending to bring Fran'Sheila and Ace back together. Fran'Sheila's words about Ace's riches stimulated Leticia's thoughts. *Maybe she'll give me half of what Ace is going to give her or something,* she thinks to herself. *Or maybe Ace might be so happy that the baby is not mine and pay me for all of this. He was sleeping in my bed. I'ma let him know. I need to be compensated for something. For my time. Since he got all this money,* Leticia says this to herself as Fran'Sheila continues to talk about how fortunate she is in life. *I'm doing all of this matchmaking and making everybody else happy, and I'll still be living in the ghetto. Maybe they shouldn't be together. I didn't tell Ace who the mother was. I just told him that he had a son. I should be the one that gets treated like a queen, not her.*

Leticia blocks out all of Fran'Sheila's conversation while having second thoughts as she contemplates on her riches. *If I just shoot this girl, it would be as if the baby was mine. I could adopt the boy and let Ace take a paternity test to prove that the baby is his, and then he'll put a ring on my finger. Ace don't even know that she's coming and don't know that it's her baby neither.*

With each rest stop, a different concept is in her head about how to become an instant millionaire by way of excluding Fran'Sheila as a parent. She didn't have a gun to shoot her with. *If I crashed this car, everybody in the car might die, unless they're wearing their seat belts,* she thinks while still vexing. As Leticia glances at Fran'Sheila, then at Diamond through the rearview mirror, she notices that they are wearing seat belts. In the late evening, Leticia decides to pull into the rest stop to take a nap. As they approach the state of Georgia, Leticia decides to have a fresh start before reaching the city of Atlanta. The short nap Leticia wanted to take takes hours. Leticia's continuance of driving, and her heavy thoughts of getting paid, drains her mentally.

After freshening up and changing the baby's diaper early Monday morning, the drive continues. Leticia agrees to meet Ace around 12:00 p.m. The closer to Atlanta they are, the less Leticia's hopes are of becoming a queen. As stated, desperate times calls for desperate measures. Leticia decides to crash the car and say that another car cut her off the road. Her other option is that a deer ran in front of her and she tried to avoid it and ran into the bridge. Leticia wants the speed to be between sixty-five and seventy upon impact on the bridge. Diamond is snuggled in tightly in the baby's seat. Fran'Sheila is strapped in her seat too with her seat belt on. Leticia decides to unbuckle Fran'Sheila's seat belt as she sleeps without waking her as she drives the car. The release button is on the top, so it is easy access to it.

The sun begins to rise and another dilemma develops. *What bridge would be the right bridge to hit?* she thinks to herself. Leticia practices in her mind how she would crash the car as she approaches underpass after underpass of bridges. Money and fortune dominate her thoughts, and there is only one obstacle that is keeping her from it, and that obstacle is in the passenger's seat. Leticia approaches the next underpass with speed at seventy miles per hour as Fran'Sheila and the baby sleep. Leticia's heart is pounding faster as she reaches over with her right hand to push down on the release button of Fran'Sheila's seat belt. After pushing down on the button, the seat belt slowly retracts into its slot. While the belt is moving across Fran'Sheila's chest, she slowly wakes from the movement of the seat belt. Leticia swerves out of the right lane and into the shoulder of the road. She drives onto the grass and hits the concrete beam that is holding the bridge. Upon impact, Leticia's arm hits the steering wheel just before the airbag deploys. As the airbag deploys, it hits Leticia's face, knocking her unconscious as she hit the back of her head on the headrest. Fran'Sheila's body ejects from the car through the passenger window as her airbag deploys. And the baby awakens from the crash and begins to cry as he remains tightly snuggled in his baby' seat.

The following day on Tuesday, the crash is reported on the front page of the Atlanta newspaper. Ace sees the article but doesn't read it because it is another auto accident among many that happen every day. Besides, he hardly knows anyone in Atlanta. If fights or shootings occurred and they made the headlines, those are what draws his attention. Since the arrival of his child never materialized, Ace devoted his attention back to his schoolwork. He did call Leticia a few times that day, not knowing that she is hospitalized in the same city he is in.

Leticia is convalescing from a sprained arm and a headache. The car is totaled from the crash. Late Tuesday morning, as Leticia lies in her hospital bed, gaining her consciousness, she has no idea of what happened or why she is there. When Leticia calls for the nurse, the nurse calls the doctor. The doctor walks into the room with the hospital chaplain to console her. As they approach her, the doctor holds the morning newspaper in his hand and has a stern look on his face.

"Good morning, young lady. How are you feeling?"

"Sore," she says, still a bit confused.

"Well, you were in a car accident and bruised your arm. You were unconscious at the scene, and your seat belt saved your life." The doctor pauses for a few seconds after telling her what he thinks is the good news. After taking a deep breath, the doctor continues, "Unfortunately, your friend, Fran'Sheila, died at the scene of the accident."

Leticia is wondering about what car accident she was in and why Fran'Sheila was with her. The doctor tells Leticia what hospital she is in and tells her his name. He smiles at Leticia as he tells her, "But there is more good news to this. Besides the seat belt saving your life, the car seat that your baby was in also saved his life. Yes! Your baby was firmly strapped in. He's in the nursery doing just fine. If there's anything else you need, let the nurse or me know. We'll be glad to help you. The police will be in here soon to talk to you about the accident, so get some more rest until they get here."

The doctor put the newspaper on the table next to Leticia, smiles, and walks out with the chaplain. The impact of what happened does not really hit her yet. Leticia doesn't even know that she has a baby until the doctor gives her one with his words. It all seems like a dream to her. Leticia knows that Fran'Sheila hates her. Leticia knows that she doesn't own a car. And she knows that she doesn't have a baby. *He must have the wrong patient*, she thinks to herself. *There must be another reason why this bandage is on my arm. Maybe I fell or something. Or it's just a bad dream.* With that last thought, she goes back to sleep.

After spending two days in the hospital with questionings from the Georgia State Police and the sheriff's department, Leticia makes arrangements with her friend, Cynthia Taylor, to take the amtrak train back home. While at home, Leticia collects donations and makes arrangements for Fran'Sheila's funeral. It is a private viewing and burial because Fran'Sheila was not a popular girl who had many friends. Fran'Sheila's mother died earlier, and she is the only child with no father in sight. The word in the hood is that Fran'Sheila died in a car accident, but no one seems to care.

Bayshawn hears about the accident but doesn't hear that Leticia or the baby was in the car. Leticia puts the word out about the car crash; however, she doesn't mention her involvement in the crash as if she wasn't even there. Leticia makes arrangements to adopt the child with one of her friends that works at the adoption agency. Each day, Leticia parades Diamond just about everywhere she goes. She is proud to make a candid statement that Ace is Diamond's father. These words are said with much conviction because it was indeed true. The anticipation for the arrival of Leticia and Diamond and their failure to show makes Ace wonder if it is all a hoax, so Ace gets in touch with Bayshawn to ask about Leticia.

"What's good, yo? You said we were going to stay in touch with each other. I've been trying to holla at you for a minute now. I gave you my number. Do you still have it?"

When Ace is eager to know the answer to a question, he asks them in multiples so that he can get at least one satisfying answer.

"I didn't forget your number, Ace. I was going to holla at you when I got a chance. I set up a business in Harlem, selling clothes on 125th Street. So if you need to upgrade your look, you know where I'm at. But my bad for not calling."

Ace is about to ask Bayshawn another question when Bayshawn cuts him off and asks, "Did you hear about Fran'Sheila, yo?" Before Ace can answer that, Bayshawn tells him, "She died in a car accident a couple of weeks ago. I ain't never seen her drive a car before. I didn't know she had a car."

Ace remains silent for a while as Bayshawn continues to talk. "I would usually see her every now and then pushing somebody's baby around the neighborhood. But I never saw a car in her driveway. Her funeral was four days ago. But, Ace, bust this. Check it. The strange part about this is Leticia was collecting donations for her and made all of the funeral arrangements, yo. My mom told me that. As much hate those two had for each other. Something doesn't sound right with that picture."

Ace remains silent as Bayshawn continues. "She probably did it for the insurance money. Leticia is always hustling for some money from somebody. She got mad game. That's why I don't trust her, Ace. She tried to holla at me. But I'm up on her. Leticia wanted to ride shotgun in my Jag. I told her no. She just wanted to front with me. So now she's hating on me. But it's all good. I'm still getting paid."

Bayshawn pauses to think about Fran'Sheila and Ace before saying, "I'm going to let you go, Ace, so that you can reflect on things."

"No, I'll be all right in a minute. There are just a lot of things that's on my mind right now. Leticia called me last month and said that I got her pregnant. She said the baby was four months old and his name is Diamond. Leticia was supposed to come down to Atlanta a couple of weeks ago with the baby but never came. We were going to take a blood test because I don't remember making no baby."

"Four months old?" Bayshawn asks with doubt. "So you must have gotten with her about a year and a half ago."

"I don't remember getting with her at all, Bayshawn."

Bayshawn laughs at that. "Were you drunk or sleepwalking?"

Ace tells him, "All I know is when I woke up, she was standing on the side of the bed with a towel wrapped around her."

"Then you must have done something and went back to sleep, Ace."

"Well, we'll find out with the blood test. Have you seen Leticia?"

"Yeah, I've seen her with a baby, but I didn't know that the baby was yours."

"I didn't know that either," Ace says slowly.

"So all of this happened the night at Isaiah's house?"

"Yes," Ace answers.

"And you never got with her any other time after that?"

"No," Ace answers.

"Let me get back at you later, Ace. I got to check some things out, yo." They hang the phones up simultaneously. Bayshawn shakes his head from side to side, thinking, somehow, Leticia's brother Isaiah told her about the money they betted with, and now she wants to get paid. Bayshawn perceives Leticia would demand child support from Ace. But child support isn't enough for her. She is the type of lady that has to have it all. Bayshawn knows that she is about game. And Ace is a cash flow for her pockets. Leticia's attempt to get with Bayshawn in the past makes him aware of what she is about. Bayshawn knows that Leticia isn't putting time into anything that she wouldn't benefit from. Leticia is about the money. Bayshawn obliges himself to get involved with her scheme.

Now, he feels that she has just pushed up on his boy Ace to get paid.

As Bayshawn reflects on the overnight-stay incident, he remembers waking up when Leticia enters the house and seeing Fran'Sheila going upstairs. *Ace had enough time to have sobered up to know what was happening, if anything happened at all,* he thinks to himself. *Maybe she came home drunk and thought they did something. It's got to be somebody else's baby, and she can't find the baby's daddy.* He knows that the times doesn't add up. From the time Leticia ran upstairs to the time Fran'Sheila went upstairs. The "wham, bam, thank-you, ma'am" comes to his mind but fades, knowing that after having a hangover, you don't really feel like being bothered.

CHAPTER 9

Bayshawn decides to investigate the entire incident. Knowing that Leticia was away on a bus trip, she didn't come home until he saw her that morning. He also overheard the conversation Leticia had with her brother about running late for work before she entered the house. Leticia's brother Isaiah is still in the military and can't be reached by phone. Bayshawn contacts Detective Watts from the Trenton Police Department, whom he knew from the hood, about this baby-daddy incident. His statement to her is that this mysterious child is a case of fraud and blackmail. He asks her to check in what hospital Leticia gave birth in.

A week later, this same detective informs Bayshawn that, within the last two years, Leticia was not admitted to any hospital in New Jersey. Detective Watts's words reinforced Bayshawn's belief about Leticia's manipulation. He feels relief knowing that his suspicions are true until the thought of home delivery comes into his mind. That leaves him more perplexed. *Who helped deliver the baby? Did she call Fran'Sheila? As much as they hated each other, that don't even sound right.* Those questions leave him puzzled. Bayshawn's propensity for the truth transforms him into a self-made private investigator. His only aspiration is for him to expose Leticia and to protect his boy Ace. Somehow, Bayshawn thinks that if Leticia would in some way influence Ace to talk about the way Ace got his riches, Ace would expose Bayshawn's riches as well. So he went to the police station again to talk to Detective Watts. Bayshawn asks her to check the hospital maternity wards in Pennsylvania and other states in the country to see if Leticia was admitted for child delivery.

Out of curiosity, Ace makes his way back to New Jersey from his home in Georgia. The girl he loved died, and the one that he showed no interest to is now a part of his life. Ace visits Leticia first to confirm his parental status. Leticia convinces him by comparing all of Diamond's facial features that left no doubt that the baby is his. Ace promises to be a good father and wants to be a part of Diamond's life. Ace even talks about marriage so that Diamond can have his last name.

"Get married," she says, shaking her head from side to side. "I just need some money for taking care of your baby. How do you come up with this marriage thing? I think you're going too fast with this. Is this what you wanted to do with your last girlfriend? Have a baby and get married? I ain't about all that. I just want to get paid, that's all."

Ace is a little confused when he asks, "What do you mean get paid?" He says this with a disgusted look on his face. "It's not all about money. It's about family and love for the baby too."

"I know, that's right," Leticia says after hearing his words. Leticia ponders the words Fran'Sheila said about Ace's desire to marry the mother of his first child. And with this marriage, she will be living as a queen.

"Well, I mean, it takes a lot to raise a baby nowadays. I can't do it all by myself. I'm about family and stuff like that too! But let's go slow with this so it could be right," she says calmly, hoping that her words won't interfere with her getting paid. Bayshawn receives a call from Detective

Watts from the Trenton Police Department. She tells him that within the last five years, the only hospital Leticia was admitted to was in the state of Georgia, about a month ago.

"Hello, Bayshawn, this is Detective Watts. I got some information for you. Your friend Leticia was admitted into a hospital in Georgia a month ago, recovering from a car accident."

Bayshawn responds by saying, "It seems like someone you know is always in a car accident."

"Yes, from the hospital report, she and her son survived the accident, but her friend was ejected from the vehicle and died."

"That's the baby daddy," Bayshawn shouts. "Who was her friend that died? Did her friend live in Georgia? Maybe he is the baby's pappy," Bayshawn states this, hoping that he finally found the real baby's daddy. "No, the passenger of the car is not the baby's pappy," the detective says while giggling.

Bayshawn says with excitement, disputing her in hopes that he is right, "I think he is the father. They all went on vacation together. Ain't no telling what else they could have done together."

"Well, Bayshawn, the passenger was a woman, so that's not possible now, is it?"

After thinking about it, Bayshawn replies, "Oh, I thought we had something. Was the woman her cousin or something? Was she from down there or from Trenton? What's the lady's name, Detective?"

"Fran'Sheila Smith," is her reply.

Those words hit Bayshawn like a Mack truck going one hundred miles per hour. The more information Bayshawn receives about Leticia, the more mystified he becomes. Bayshawn is not aware that Leticia and Fran'Sheila became friends before they drove to Georgia.

What were they doing in Georgia? Was Fran'Sheila kidnapped? he asks himself. "Those two hated each other, Detective. Something ain't right. This don't look good." He couldn't fathom two enemies in a car on the road to Georgia with a baby.

Bayshawn thanks the detective for the information and slowly hangs up the phone. Detective Watts continues her investigation into the birth of Diamond based on the information she just received from Bayshawn and finds no records of the child's birth by Leticia. So she turns her attention toward the Missing Child's Bureau and adoption agencies for an answer. This shocking news of the way Fran'Sheila died made Bayshawn more vexed with Leticia. Wondering why Leticia wasn't the one to die in the car accident, ejected from the car, he says out loud to himself, "She killed her. I know she did. She must have pushed her out of the car or something. Why was Fran'Sheila the only one that died?" Those questions Bayshawn asks himself over and over again. But he is never able to develop an answer.

When Ace finally meets up with Bayshawn, he tells him about his visit with Leticia and her son. Bayshawn is still vexed about the fact that Leticia was with Fran'Sheila when she died and is upset that Ace isn't trying to find out what really caused the accident.

"What makes you think that's really your son, yo?"

"The baby got my eyes, my nose, and his hair is a little curly like my hair was when I was little too!"

"Ace those looks could change as he gets older. Any baby could look like anybody when they're young like that. You just can't claim a baby 'cause he looks like you."

With the euphoria in his mind, Ace tells him, "Well, I'm convinced that's my little dude, and I'm marrying her."

Bayshawn pauses after hearing those words, then asks, "Marrying who?"

"I'm marrying my baby's momma."

"So now she's making you marry her?"

"No, I asked her to marry me. But she said she didn't want to rush into it right now. I know you think I'm crazy. I just want our son to have a mother and father that's married, that's all. My son would have my last name, and the whole world would know that he's my dude, my firstborn."

Bayshawn knows how stubborn Ace can get when he thinks he's right. He reflects on the time he told Ace that hanging with Rock would get him killed, and Ace ignored Bayshawn's warning. He doesn't want to argue with Ace, knowing that Ace is caught up in the moment with his little dude. So Bayshawn conceives of a way to prove that the little dude is not Ace's and, at the same time, expose Leticia as a manipulative con artist who got mad game.

"Okay, Ace, that sounds good. I'm sure the whole world would want to know," Bayshawn says sarcastically. "But let's do it like this. I'll make the arrangement for the both of you to get a DNA test in New York. I'll get in touch with the *Maury* show. They do those kinds of things. They'll have the two of you on TV. And as y'all sit on TV, they'll read the results to you. In that way, over fifty million viewers will hear the results too."

"Hey, Bayshawn, that will work. Bust this, my first child in view of TV with the whole world watching, no doubt."

"But, Ace, don't tell Leticia that I'm setting her up." After thinking about what he's just said, Bayshawn tells him, "Uh, I mean, setting this thing up for y'all. Tell her it's your idea."

"No, doubt, Bayshawn."

"When are you leaving to go back to Georgia?"

"I'm leaving tomorrow morning."

"All right, holla at me before you bounce."

Ace departs from Bayshawn to tell Leticia about this good news.

The next day while working in New York, Bayshawn contacts the *Maury* show to arrange for the DNA appearance. Next, he calls the Trenton Police Station to consult with Detective Watts about Fran'Sheila's death. Bayshawn is staying on top of this to procure any information that will implicate Leticia. He embellishes the accident scene to the detective and reaches his own conclusion.

"Hello, Detective Watts, I'm inquiring about the accident again. Could Fran'Sheila have been murdered at the scene and then the accident was staged as a cover-up?"

"I don't think so, Bayshawn."

"Was the passenger's seat belt broken or defective or something?"

"That's not in the report that I got. All it said was she wasn't wearing a seat belt."

"What time of day was the accident?"

"Approximately eight a.m. according to the report."

"Is it possible, Detective, for you to ask them to check the vehicle for a defective seat belt? And if there wasn't a defective seat belt, ask them to check and see whose fingerprints was the last one to push the seat belt release button, please. Leticia might have pushed the release button, then crashed the car."

Detective Watts has no motive for a murder in this accident, so she states, "Bayshawn, there's no indication if either one of them was the last to push the release button."

"Detective, if the fingerprints are pointed towards the passenger's seat or if the thumbprint is on top of Fran'Sheila's print, then that is an indication that Leticia was the last one to push the release button. I won't put nothing past her. I don't trust her."

Detective Watts becomes a little annoyed with these questions and asks, "There's no motive for a murder, is there?"

"The motive for the murder could be hate because they hated each other. Fran'Sheila must have known that the baby wasn't Ace's little dude, and Leticia thought Fran'Sheila was going to tell Ace. That's why Leticia killed her." Bayshawn says this with much confidence. His persuasive words convince the detective to continue her investigation into Fran'Sheila's death.

"Bayshawn, I'll talk to the Georgia State Police and look into all of this a little further and get back with you."

Bayshawn conjectures up this version of the accident in hopes that Detective Watts might have seen these kinds of accidents before. He begins to investigate also by talking to two of Leticia's closest confidants, Sharian Mackins and Dorothy Stephens, to see what they knew about the child. He's determined to find out the truth because nothing makes sense out of this whole scenario.

Weeks pass, and there is no new information that is essential to Bayshawn's accusation about Leticia. The anticipation of more information that isn't coming to him from the street is frustrating Bayshawn. So he calls the police detective again for any findings. She informs him that Leticia's fingerprints were on the passenger's seat release button. Detective Watts states that it's still speculation, and his case against her is weak. Bayshawn argues that Leticia is trying to extort money from Ace with a baby that's not his, and Fran'Sheila knows about it so that's why Leticia killed her.

"Why doesn't your friend take this to court and file a motion for a DNA test."

"I got in touch with a TV show in New York that gives DNA testing and broadcasts the results live. I'm waiting for the paperwork and for them to get in touch with both parties. Then we'll go from there, Detective."

"Okay, keep me informed."

This new information is conducive to his case against Leticia. His suspicions grow even stronger. Bayshawn spends more time stalking Leticia. He calls Ace to see if Ace received the papers to sign for the TV appearance. Ace's response is yes.

While stalking Leticia's daily routine, Bayshawn notices that her personality does not indicate anything unusual. In fact, it basically consists of working and shopping. Meanwhile, Detective Watts gets in touch with the *Maury* show in New York to confirm a DNA test for Ace and Leticia. She obtains a copy of the adoption papers for Leticia for a baby named Diamond. Whiteout covers the mother's real name, and the word "unknown" is typed over it. Leticia's friend at the agency changed the paperwork for her. The detective also discloses information to the police in Georgia about a fraudulent police statement by Leticia concerning the accident. She relinquishes the information to the state police, provided to her by Bayshawn, about Fran'Sheila knowing that Ace isn't the baby's father. Therefore, Leticia had to kill her because Fran'Sheila was going to expose the truth to Ace about who the real father of Diamond is. Although Detective Watts is skeptical about this motive, she decides to go with it, knowing that accidents occur every day.

The detective requests for DNA samples from Fran'Sheila's body from the Georgia State Police so that she can have DNA samples from all parties involved. Fran'Sheila's body will have to be exhumed while Ace, Leticia, and the baby's blood will be taken from the studios in New York. Detective Watts explains her suspicions to the director of the show, and the director relays that information to the technician who is taking blood from all parties involved. The technician agrees to manipulate Leticia so she wouldn't have a change of heart in appearing on the show. She receives blood and mouth swabs from Leticia but explains to Leticia that this is the way it will be administered to Ace and Diamond. The technician has to make Leticia feel comfortable that the test isn't for her. Leticia knows that the baby is Ace's flesh and blood and feels elated that this test will leave no doubt in his mind. Getting paid wouldn't be a problem for Leticia, with the presumption that Diamond is being taken care of. The dilemma the detective is now confronting is knowing that Diamond was conceived from a woman. But in this case, the question is, from which woman? After the blood and mouth swab is taken from Leticia, the technician carefully wraps it, places it into a small container, seals it, and throws it into the trash can in front of Leticia. That assures Leticia that she isn't being tested.

After Leticia exits the room, the technician removes the sample from the trash can. This sample *will* be used for DNA testing. This process is done to Ace and Diamond too on the TV studio and sent to the laboratory for results. All three parties are to return to the studio in three weeks.

Three days before the test results are given on TV, Detective Watts received the DNA results from Fran'Sheila's exhumed body in Georgia and all parties involved. Fran'Sheila and Ace's DNA match Diamond's DNA. She now has a motive for the accident—first-degree murder. Detective Watts informs the authorities in Georgia and requests for an arrest warrant from the Superior Court of the State of Georgia. The court issues a warrant for the first-degree murder and fraud. She keeps this information from Bayshawn in fear of it being leaked and Leticia not showing up for her TV appearance. Detective Watts wants Leticia to further incriminate herself by her words or actions on the show. This will strengthen her case.

Leticia is certain of the test results. She has no doubts about who the father is. Her mind is on her fame and fortune. Leticia is even contemplating marriage to ensure one big happy family. This seems so surreal to her. This is her opportunity to become a housewife and leave the hood for a better life. Leticia's confidence allows her to become bodacious in her conversations with Ace, demanding more material possessions and money. Her suggestion for the baby's transportation is a new Jaguar car in her name. Out of jealousy, she wants everything Fran'Sheila would have procured if she were alive today. But Leticia feels that she is better than Fran'Sheila, so she wants all that and more.

Ace is shocked to hear her say he must move away from his home in Georgia and back to New Jersey. From there, he can live with his new family. Leticia tells Ace that her job is interfering with her parent time in raising Diamond, and she needs to quit working to nurse the baby. Their new home, as Leticia informs Ace, has to be a mansion with a big backyard in the suburbs. She describes how she will decorate the home and furnish it with Italian furniture and with Persian carpets in each room. Ace's acquiescence allows her to believe that he approves of all those demands. That gives him second thoughts about fatherhood. College is the utmost important part of his life as he reminisces on Fran'Sheila's words about getting that paper, meaning that diploma for life. And he is more determined to complete college without interference. Any change in his college decisions will be based on the outcome of the paternity test.

On the day before the TV appearance, Ace checks into his hotel room provided by the *Maury* show in New York. Leticia checks into a separate hotel in the city. Both receive a thousand dollars spending money and special accommodations. Ace calls Bayshawn from his hotel room to ask if he is coming.

"What's good, Bayshawn?"

"God is good. Where you at, Ace?"

"They got me in this plush hotel with a view of the whole city. You coming up?"

Bayshawn feels a little at ease that Ace is in New York. Now he hopes Leticia will show up.

"I'm in Trenton. I'll be up. The *Maury* show gave me a front-row seat for calling the show for y'all and putting this whole thing together. Hey, Ace, are you with Leticia?"

"No, I don't know where she's at. They said we will be separated until the show. I think she's at another hotel."

"That's all good. That way, y'all could remain separated after the show too."

"That all depends on the outcome of the test, Bayshawn."

"Yo, you buggin'. You going to marry her after the show, for real?"

"If the test results are positive, I'm going to propose right there on the stage at the show."

"Ace, you should propose to her during the commercial so that you won't play yourself in view of all the millions of people that will be watching the show."

"How will I be playing myself by getting married?"

"First, you said you ain't did nothing with her, and now you're saying if the test result is positive. You're lying to me, Ace. I think you've been creeping with her, and now you act like you don't know what's up. You can't play me, yo," Bayshawn says, disgusted. "Hey, Ace, I'll holla at you at the show tomorrow."

Ace is too confused to talk, so they hang up the phones without Ace saying another word.

The next day at the show, Leticia walks into the studio smiling as she pushes Diamond in his stroller. She acts as if this is a new life for her. She socializes with all the staff members, telling them that Ace is the father and that they are getting married today. Bayshawn walks into the studio, mad about the situation, knowing how Ace lied to him about Leticia, thinking to himself how Leticia was hating on him while all the time Ace was feeling her.

Ace comes into the studio and remains separated from Leticia in the guest room. Detective Watts is in company of a state police detective from Georgia and a New York City police detective behind the stage, awaiting Leticia's arrival on stage. There are other guests on the show for test results too. The producer scheduled for Ace's results to be read last.

There is drama by the men who are challenging their so-called baby momma's. The guest prior to Leticia allows the host to display a little sense of sarcasm. The guest named Maurice is positive that he isn't the father because he is the fourth man that this woman brought to this show for testing, trying to find her baby's daddy. Maurice is confident and sure that this woman got him confused with somebody else as she desperately searches for the father. Maurice takes his hat off and walks over to the picture screen that has the little boy on display. The screen displays Maurice and a little baby named Troy with both their pictures side by side. As he points to the screen, he says, "This boy don't look nothing like me. My hair is not curly like his. This boy is light-skinned and my complexion is dark. Plus his nose is pointy." Maurice looks at the host of the show and tells him, "That baby looks more like you than he does me." Maurice starts laughing as he asks the host, "Have you two met somewhere before?"

The host briefly looks at the woman, then back at Maurice. Maurice continues and says, "But serious, does this baby look anything like me?"

The host responds, "No, he doesn't."

"Do you think that this is my baby?" Maurice asks.

"Yes," the host tells him with a smile.

"How can you say that when nothing on that boy looks like me? Aren't I the fourth man to be tested for this baby?"

"Yes, you are, and I can explain why I think you're the father without me even reading the results."

Maurice sits down next to the baby's mother (his accuser) on stage and listens as the host speaks facetiously and asks, "What is your nickname, Maurice?"

"My nickname is Moe. They call me Moe."

"Well, Maurice, that's how the baby's father is going to be chosen today. Three other men were tested, and you're the forth. We've tested Eenie, then we tested Meenie, and we've tested Miney, and now you, Moe." The host begins to smile as he opens the envelope and says, "For some strange reason, it's always Moe." As he reads the letter from the envelope, it read, "When it comes to the DNA test of little Troy, Maurice, you are the father."

Maurice put his head down in shame and walks off the stage. Leticia is called to enter the stage next. The audience applauds for her as she walks onto the stage. She acts like a proud mother who is about to prove to the world that, once again, she is right. Without sitting down, she walks right to the TV monitor on the wall displaying Diamond's and Ace's faces. The similarities are there.

"Tell me this ain't his baby," she shouts. "If you tell me this ain't his child, I'll call you a liar." She continues, "The hair, the eyes. Look at the nose! Y'all see it. Don't y'all see it?"

The audience agrees with applause and cheers.

"And after the results come in, I'm going to get mine. That's right. I'm going to get paid."

Bayshawn is sitting in the front row, questioning himself if she knows anything about the money Ace made from his illegal bet, and if Ace is lying about not being the father. As Leticia continues to brag about herself, Bayshawn looks to his left and sees Detective Watts standing in the corner with two cops. He's puzzled by the sight of her. But he thinks, if Ace is not the father, Leticia might get arrested based on what he told her, he hopes. So now he feels a little better listening to her talk.

"Why does Ace have doubts that this is his child?" the host asks.

"He said because he's in college, and he's not ready to be a father now."

"Didn't he have nine months to get ready to be a father?" the host asks as he giggles.

"He should have. But if he did or didn't, today is graduation day," she says with much certainty. "And I would like to say something to all of the fathers and the future fathers out there too." Leticia stands up from her seat and bounces her head up and down as she walks toward the audience while still on stage. Leticia addresses the men in the audience with an attitude as she speaks. She raises her left hand to get the audience's full attention and says, "To all of the men out there, if you're not ready to become a father, then don't lie in a father's position. Ladies, holla if you hear me."

All the women stand up from their seats and cheer as they give her a standing ovation. Leticia walks off the stage to greet some of the audience with high fives and handshakes as they cheer in agreement. The men boo her and tell her to sit down, displaying their disagreement to what she said. Leticia walks back to her seat as the ladies in the audience continue to cheer for her. She unofficially has become the spokeswoman for all the fathers in the world.

The host of the show now introduces Ace to the stage. He walks onto the stage in the midst of boos. Ace is nervous but excited as he walks to his seat. The host asks him if he thinks the baby is his child. Ace tells him Diamond looks a little like him.

"What do you mean a little like you?" Leticia snaps. "Everything in him is you. And you're going to come here on TV in front of the world and say he looks a little like you. He is you."

The audience shouts and applauds. Bayshawn is looking convinced that Diamond does look like Ace too but is hoping otherwise so Leticia can get arrested. Leticia continues to shout on stage, claiming how all the men who came on stage had doubts and were told the truth. She says all she wants is to be respected and treated like a queen. The audience agrees with her and applauds.

The host grabs the envelope with the results in it. He raises it up high to show the audience and says, "We will see if you deserve to be treated like a queen."

As the audience claps, the host asks Ace that if the baby is his child, would he be in the child's life? Ace's response is, "If she's the mother of my son, I'll be in both of their lives. And yes, she'll be my queen too."

Bayshawn looks at him as if he is crazy for making a statement like that. The host opens the envelope and says, "When it comes to the paternity of baby Diamond, Ace, you are the father!"

Out of contempt, Bayshawn's heart feels as if it dropped to his stomach. "Yes, yes!" Leticia shouted. "I told you! I told you," she said, knowing that her plan has worked, and she'll be living happily ever after. "Now give me mine. That's right. Give me mine!"

Ace is too embarrassed to look at Bayshawn, who is sitting right in front of him. He's feeling guilty but proud that he has a son. Staff members bring Diamond on to the stage and give him to Ace to hold while sitting.

"That's your flesh and blood," Leticia says, feeling proud for what she has accomplished. "That's your flesh and blood. And there's no doubt about that."

As Ace holds his son while sitting, Bayshawn now knows that Ace lied to him about Leticia and knows that he can't be trusted anymore. After Ace kisses the baby, he stands up to hand Diamond over to the host of the show. Ace reaches into his pocket and pulls out a diamond ring. Bayshawn tells him as he sat in his seat not to do it. But Ace is determined as he stands in front of Leticia and begins to kneel down on one knee to propose. The audience cheer. Bayshawn takes three steps toward Ace and yells, "Don't put that on her finger. What are you doing?"

"He's doing what he's supposed to be doing," Leticia yells back. The show's host stands up and grabs another envelope, raising it high to the audience, and says, "And here's a second test result from the test."

Bayshawn turns and walks away from the stage, feeling disappointed and disgusted, so he begins to leave. He has heard and seen enough, knowing that Ace lied to him.

Leticia stands up while Ace is still kneeling and shouts at Bayshawn as he walks away, "What? What? Don't leave now, punk. You heard the results. I heard you've been asking Dorothy and Sharian about me. You wanted to know the truth, so you got the truth. Come back and take this paper home with you before you leave. The truth hurts, don't it?" She shouts these words as she walks to the edge of the stage, pointing at him. Ace is having a difficult time on stage trying to put the ring on her finger as she continues to move with excitement. Also, Ace has never bought a ring for a lady before, so evidently, the ring is too small and doesn't fit the appropriate finger.

Leticia's attention is focused on Bayshawn and what he told Ace not to do. She thinks that this second test result the host is holding is a copy of the first result to back up the test. With this confidence of who the father is, Leticia shouts out to Bayshawn as he turns to walk up the aisle. As Bayshawn turns to go up the aisle, he notices Detective Watts from Trenton. His theory of Leticia blackmailing Ace is shattered by the test. While her left arm is stretched in Ace's direction, Ace is still attempting to place the ring on her finger. Leticia ignores Ace as she leans toward her right to taunt Bayshawn as he walk.

"Come back and take this test result with you before you leave. So when you see me walking on the blocks in the hood, looking good, you can bow down to this queen. You can tell all the rest of the haters around the way when you see them that I'm getting mine," she says this while raising her right hand above her head, pointing her finger at Bayshawn sideways in a gangsta fashion. "Listen to this announcement again before you leave," she shouted. "Come back and get your copy so you can hang it on your wall. Where you going? Come get your copy before you leave. And don't think that you're going to be the godfather of my baby, punk."

Bayshawn ignores her and continues to slowly walk. Bayshawn feels like running out of the auditorium, but his legs are too heavy from feeling embarrassed. Besides feeling embarrassed, he is angry at both of them. Leticia's irritating voice compels Bayshawn to briefly stop and turn around so that he could responds to his enemy. He wants to tell her something about herself before he walks out. Bayshawn glances at Detective Watts, knowing that he doesn't have a case against Leticia, so he turns back around and continues to walk.

Leticia smiles at him, feeling content that she got her point across. She points two fingers sideways in front of her chest, indicating a peace sign and hollers, "Deuces."

Ace is about to put the ring on her pinkie finger, just so that it can be on her hand because it's too small for the appropriate finger, but changes his mind. Ace slowly stands up from kneeling with the ring in his hand and stares at the ring while still holding Leticia's left hand. Since Leticia isn't concerned about the ring, he doesn't put it on any finger but just holds it in his hand. The ring isn't even on Leticia's mind. Euphoria is what she is feeling, and at the same time, she takes advantage on national TV to express herself to all her enemies that are hating on her from the hood. And Bayshawn is the only one in the audience at the time.

"When it comes to the maternity test results from the DNA test of little Diamond," the host states out loud as Bayshawn is eight steps from the exit door. Leticia looks at the host with her eyes wide open. She leans toward her right as Ace holds her left hand, then she poses with her right hand up to her ear to hear the announcement more clearly and says to the announcer, "Holla."

"Leticia, you are **not** the mother of this child." The host states these words as he holds the papers up over his head, showing it to the audience. Bayshawn stops in his tracks as he pushes the door open with his right hand. The sounds of oohs and aahs echo from the audience as he stands between the doors and holds the door open with his right hand. Pandemonium fills the audience as he turns around slowly toward his left, still holding on to the door with his right hand. Bayshawn watches as Detective Watts and the two cops walk onto the stage together. The detective has an arrest warrant in her hand as one of the officers pull out his handcuffs.

"Leticia, I'm Detective Watts from the Trenton Police Department. I have a warrant for your arrest for the murder of Fran'Sheila Smith."

"She's not the mother?" Ace shouts with disbelief to the host. "What do you mean she's not the mother? That baby looks just like us."

The detective continues, "You have the right to remain silent," as the officers attempt to place the cuffs on Leticia.

"No, no, no," Leticia hollers while covering her face with both of her hands as she tilts her head forward. She begins to flail her arms to avoid the arrest, knowing that her whole world has just been turned upside down. "She's not the mother? Am I'm the father? Who did she murder? Where's the mother?" Ace continues to ask, still in a world of confusion.

Bayshawn begins to walk back toward the stage.

"Anything you say may be used against you in a court of law," the detective adamantly states. "You have a right to an attorney."

"No, no," Leticia cries.

Ace impatiently waits for an answer. "I'm not the father. Who's the mother?" Ace asks.

Bayshawn slowly walks back toward the stage, trying desperately to hear what she's being charged with.

"No, it was an accident," Leticia continues to cry out loud.

As Bayshawn walks toward the stage, Ace asks him, "Who she killed?"

"If you can't afford an attorney, one would be appointed for you by the court of law," the detective said.

Bayshawn walks onto the stage and holds Diamond in his arms. Detective Watts informs Ace that the baby is Fran'Sheila's son. She tells him that Leticia is charged with first-degree murder of Fran'Sheila.

"The crash was deliberate murder. Motivated by jealousy and greed. Come to the Trenton Police Department for my report."

Bayshawn walks off the stage, relieved that there won't be a marriage between the two, as Leticia is still crying onstage in handcuffs.

After the show, Ace and Bayshawn leave together with Diamond wrapped in Ace's arms. Bayshawn takes Ace to a kids' store up the avenues in New York City that sells car seat for little babies. This seat is a necessity for the long journey home. The car seat will be the first of many items Ace will purchase for his son as he enters fatherhood.

Bayshawn isn't in any position to tell Ace what to do as a father since he isn't one. But the only two pieces of advice that he stresses to Ace are, "Diapers, you got to keep getting diapers, yo. And milk. They always got to drink milk. It's like when it goes into their mouth, the milk goes straight into their diapers. That's when they start crying because they want you to pat them on the back and compliment them for not keeping the milk in them. Then after you compliment them with the pats, they go to sleep. So that's what you got to do now, Ace."

Ace looks at him for a second and says, "Bayshawn, you stupid."

"Naw, Ace, feel me on this. We keep giving them bottles of milk when they're babies, and when they get grown, they start drinking forty-ounce bottles of beer. They start holding bottles up to their mouths at a young age, Ace. Somebody needs to do something about that."

As they leave New York City, they discuss the early-morning sleepover at Leticia's house, concluding that nothing did happen between the two. Realizing he needs to be a leader in leading his little dude into manhood, Ace still feels the need for that bond with Fran'Sheila.

The next day, Ace locates the gravestone of Fran'Sheila and visits it with Diamond. Fran'Sheila's gravestone has a picture of her face engraved on it. Ace's new challenge in life is to raise a child with no mother and no experience. It won't be as difficult as it seems because he can always depend on his mom for assistance.

Ace kneels on one knee and talks to the gravestone for a few minutes as he stares at Fran'Sheila's eyes in the picture on the gravestone, then he begins to cry. As he reflects back on Fran'Sheila, he knows that she was that kind of girl who openly gave love to those she cared about and that she didn't deserve to die. It's peculiar how Ace provides a valuable diamond ring to a woman who is undeserving of it. The woman who did deserve the ring, unknowingly to Ace, provided a priceless, young gift for him. The only gift Ace is able to provide for Fran'Sheila now is the love and provisions he gives to his son, Diamond. As a young parent, Fran'Sheila did all that she could to provide love and affection for her son. But now that she's gone, she can't give that motherly love that the baby needs. While still kneeling, he thinks to himself that even though she is gone and there is nothing else that she can give, she gave him something precious for life: **DIAMOND**.

Edwards Brothers Malloy
Thorofare, NJ USA
February 26, 2013